M000312291

PRE-EMPTIVE STRIKE LEADERSHIP

Neutralizing Behavioral Threats That Are Infiltrating Your Organization

Dr. Arlene Battishill
AND
Michael Levitt

Copyright © 2019 Dr. Arlene Battishill and Michael Levitt

ALL RIGHTS RESERVED. This book contains material protected under International and Federal Copyright Laws and Treaties. Any unauthorized reprint or use of this material is prohibited. No part of this book may be reproduced or transmitted in any form or by any means, electronic or mechanical, including photocopying, recording, or by any information storage and retrieval system without express written permission from the author/publisher.

ISN: 978-1-64085-492-5 (Paperback)

ISBN: 978-1-64085-493-2 (Hardback)

ISBN: 978-1-64085-494-9 (Ebook)

LCCN: 2018963623

CHAPTER ONE
THE THREAT INSIDE YOUR WALLS

DON'T WORRY, THIS COULD NEVER HAPPEN TO YOU.

I t's 5am and Paul wakes to news that the organization he leads is in crisis. Overnight a couple of disgruntled employees quit by means of dramatically airing their grievances on the internet. Their titillating video went viral. Paul's cell phone is blowing up with calls from board members demanding to know how the hell this happened and what's going to be done about it. The Customer Service department is overwhelmed with canceled orders, the media is calling for official comments, while social media is abuzz with everyone's "unofficial comments" – speculative and grossly uninformed, but oh so juicy! This is all before Paul's first cup of coffee.

By the time he arrives at the office, the staff are huddled and whispering. The Human Resources Director looks like a deer caught in the headlights and has turned fifty shades of pale. The former employees' Manager is cowering in his office. The opening bell for the stock market is less than thirty minutes from ringing, and stock futures are predicting a 25% drop for the organization at market open.

An emergency meeting is called for everyone; the atmosphere in the room is toxic. The management team is visibly shaken and displaying no traces of leadership. Employees sit smugly observing the carnage, momentarily reveling in the power they feel because a couple of their own managed to bring the organization and its leadership to its knees. As Paul surveys the room, his thoughts circle back to the phone calls that started this nightmare of a day and he realizes he doesn't actually know the answer to the board members' question. He also wonders how the hell this had happened.

THE BEHAVIORAL THREATS THAT ARE INFILTRATING YOUR ORGANIZATION

You think this can't happen to you? If so, you have vastly underestimated the power of your employees. Every aspect of the story above is true, and there are countless other examples to choose from. Why? Because most organizations have failed to come to grips with the growing threat that employees represent, and have carelessly overlooked this very real liability when performing their risk assessments.

In this changing landscape of almost infinite channels of communication flow, a hunger for salacious news over facts, and the merging of personal/public/professional lives, the risks that employees represent to their organizations can rise to astronomical levels when accounting for liability, cost and distraction. Situations such as the one experienced by Paul throw organizations into the spotlight, compromising the brand and the profitability of the organization, not to mention the longevity and legacy of the founders, executives and managers.

Let us be clear: employees are not inherently your enemy. However, they do represent a very real threat that, if mishandled, can turn your employee into someone who behaves very much like the enemy. The problem is, when organizational leaders are identifying risk, there is an obsession with scanning the horizon for danger while failing to look over their shoulders at their own troops. If you wish to neutralize threats to your organization, you must possess the courage to look within your walls and learn the leadership skills to develop and deploy a targeted pre-emptive strike before it's too late. This will be your field guide.

Let's get started.

OUR MISDIRECTED VIEW OF RISK: ONLY LOOKING OUTWARDS

When most organizations analyze risk they focus primarily on threats that are clearly definable, quantifiable and measurable, and most always associated with external factors. The nature of these threats usually include economic, natural, legal, political and financial forces. Here are some examples of common "external threats" for different types of organizations (see if any of them look familiar):

Corporations are largely concerned with:

Market fluctuations; competition and consolidation; changes to federal, state and local regulations; mergers and acquisitions or divestitures; international operations; new products and services development; intellectual property infringement; economic conditions; attracting or retaining personnel; pricing pressures; margins; cost cutting; legal proceedings; cyclical revenue; product liability; quality and safety issues; supplier and vendor concerns; inability to acquire capital or financing; and predicting customer demand.

Start-ups and early-growth organizations have a focus on:

Actions that "skirt the law"; a lack of operational infrastructure; declining product and service quality; inability to capture or analyze key data quickly; inadequate due diligence; a planning horizon that is too short; loyalty to founding employees who lack accountability; organizational focus that is blurred; management practices or capabilities that are substandard; and a sense that management is untouchable.

Non-profits worry about:

Funding shortages; attracting, retaining and engaging donors; sustainability; lack of resources; injuries at special events; data breaches; volunteer injuries; government regulation and tax reform; technology and software concerns; donor fatigue or disinterest; internal or external fraud; inefficient or misuse of assets; inadequate monitoring or understanding of investments; incomplete or unreliable reporting; violation of legal requirements; government investigations or audits; market pressure; and "mission creep".

These threats are typically dealt with in the same straightforward way: hiring specific types of lawyers to deal with legal issues, accounting firms that have certain expertise, capital financing people that help navigate the economic waters, communications firms to handle unfavorable press, technology providers to deal with hackers, business analysts that assess market conditions ... and the list goes on. Most external threats can be predicted and we can plan a mitigating response to them. Straightforward problem, straightforward solution.

Internal threats, such as those posed by employees, are a different animal and rare is the leader that recognizes the full extent of the threat that employees represent, and the power that even *one* employee possesses to derail an entire organization. Part of the reason is because the problem lies in the fact that, for most organizations, "people management" is not a very sexy topic. Let's admit it - we executives are a lot more impressed by a showy display of mental gymnastics around economics and finances. And is there anything more satisfying than the sense of control we gain when strategic planning? (Let's ignore the fact that these plans are often trying to manage factors that are completely outside of our control.) Time and time again, we have witnessed employers who consider employees as little more than annoyances to be managed by Human Resources, or who dismiss "people skills" as "soft skills" – not to be respected in the real world of tough business.

Whatever the case, for the executive or leader who refuses to recognize and proactively address how potentially damaging employees can be to organizations, a world of danger awaits them. With each day that passes they come closer and closer to waking up to the same sort of phone call that started Paul's day.

TURNING OUR GAZE INWARDS: THE THREAT INSIDE YOUR WALLS

You like horses?

When was the last time you thought about the Trojan Horse? You know, the one that the Greeks left for the Trojans following ten years of battle? The Greeks, appearing to give up, sailed off into the distance and the Trojans gleefully rolled that big prized horse inside their gates. We all know how that turned out. The Trojans lowered their guard, went about their business, and out of the horse came the rest of the Greek army, who could now level the city of Troy from the inside out!

You ever hear that story and wonder, "How could they not have guessed that horse was packed full of danger? Why didn't they at least examine it a bit more closely?. Seems kinda obvious, doesn't it? Well, consider this…each of your employees has the potential to be a Trojan Horse inside the gates of your organization. All the baggage they carry with them is inside that horse, waiting to emerge and take you down the moment you stop paying attention.

They may take you down in flaming public displays such as Paul experienced, or their sabotage to your business may be more clandestine in nature, such as eroding the profitability of your organization on a da- to-day basis. In our consulting practice helping employers analyze the internal risk from employees, we have identified a list of behaviors that includes, but is not limited to:

Circulating or spreading rumors among staff, pitting employees against one another or management, encouraging bad behavior among co-workers, deliberately missing critical deadlines, lowering team morale and productivity, eroding organizational reputation to customers, making inflammatory claims, technology sabotage, financial misconduct, bodily threats, domestic terrorism, and many other behaviors that range from annoying to severe in implication.

Have we got your attention yet?

Note this - it is actually inevitable that employee behavior will be harmful to your organization; it is a question only of how harmful. The changing environment in which we operate, the changing nature of our employees drives the risk ever upwards. You need more proof? Just look at Millennials. There is nothing that brings into sharper focus the crisis of employee behavior negatively affecting organizations than examining the role Millennials play in the workforce today, as they represent the group most likely to express their discontent through public, and often devastating, means to their employer.

MILLENNIALS: OUR CHANGING WORLD, OUR CHANGING WORKFORCE, OUR ESCALATING RISK

Change is a-foot, and these feet are attached to Millennials who are marching into the workplace in greater and greater numbers. Millennials are defined by the fact that they are the most burdened and privileged generation to date. This combination of burden and privilege that they carry creates the conditions for a "perfect storm" in the environment of employment.

The burdens carried by Millennials are very real. They come to the workforce carrying a life-crushing amount of student loan debt, justifiable pessimism, and have fewer job opportunities as they compete with an aging population that is remaining employed in the top positions well past historical retirement age. When Millennials consider their future careers, they also face an entirely different employment landscape from the generations who came before. They know they will have numerous employers over their lifetime and will likely have to generate self-employment opportunities, resulting in decreased sense of loyalty or connection to one employer. This also tends to result in very little desire to "take the long view" with work since they assume they won't be around to reap the benefits of their sacrifice, energy and effort when the organization is successful. They want to benefit quickly and move up or move on. As such, they are often experienced by other staff as poor team players.

The most common criticism of Millennials? Their entitlement. They want quick results and advancement, with unrealistic returns on their work and access to power that does not reflect their experience or skills. And if they don't get what they want…watch out!

Millennials have grown up with access to technology and have a very different concept of communication. Their life-long use of communication technology means they have less barriers between their personal and public life, this includes the workplace since their professional/personal life is fused. Their instinct when upset is to share their emotions and opinions far and wide on a variety of public platforms.

Historically, employee discontent was experienced internally and rarely, if ever, made public. People within the organization might know, but certainly never outside. Today, Millennials, with their heightened sense of entitlement coupled with the prevalent use of and prominence of social media, tend to think of "going public" as a first resort instead of the last. This constitutes a public relations disaster for many organizations, even at the best of times. At the worst of times, Millennials will adopt a scorched earth policy where they'll take everyone down, and they know how to use the Internet to do it. Much as we might like them to behave differently, the reality is that this is the world we all live in now and we must come to terms with the risks inherent in that new way of life.

REMOVING THE BLINDERS

While it is the Millennials who are now commanding the attention of management with their brazen, public displays of displeasure, it should be noted that employee risk is by no means limited to Millennials. Millennials have simply forced us to pull off the blinders and recognize that there are things "going on" with our employees, and organizations must begin addressing this situation if they are going to minimize the damage that employees can inflict.

We are ringing the alarm bell for any outdated organization that thinks that employees still constitute a line on the ledger under "resources", and not an inclusion in the list of risks. We have to understand our risks. We have to understand our employees. And we have to be ready with a pre-emptive strike that can ensure the door of that Trojan Horse remains firmly shut.

The only real option available is to try and pre-empt the behavior. Anyone in business knows that success depends on "knowing your market". Well, the same goes for your employees. You want to create an effective response? You need to know what is really going on.

Let's start by looking inside those pretty wooden horses being wheeled through your lobby.

CHAPTER TWO

EXCUSE ME, CAN WE EXAMINE THE CONTENTS OF YOUR HORSE?

UNPACKING THE INVISIBLE BAGGAGE OF YOUR EMPLOYEES

Employees carry invisible baggage through the door with them every day. Packed inside are the external stressors of life, expectations and fantasies about their job, and their history with power. The contents of this invisible baggage influence an employee's reactions and behavior in the workplace. The contents may be invisible, but rest assured that there are a lot of visible clues to this baggage if you know what you're looking for. Let's start by unpacking the invisible bags.

SMUGGLING CONTRABAND PERSONAL STRESS INTO THE WORKPLACE

If you are alive, then you know that life is complicated and seems to be growing ever more so at an increasingly rapid rate. Employees have an extraordinary number of external stressors that they carry with them into the workplace on a daily basis.

The stressors that employees are experiencing fall into one of three categories: (1) trauma; (2) stress; and (3) irritation. Dealing with loved ones who are dying would fall into the trauma category. The struggles of being a single parent fall into the stress category. Dealing with rude drivers and traffic both fall into the irritation category. It can be tempting to dismiss "irritation stress", but we all know the irritation associated with driving can actually represent a significant stress upon arriving at work.

In Melanie Gordon Sheets' book *Out-of-Control: A Dialectical Behavior Therapy (DBT) - Cognitive-Behavioral Therapy (CBT) Workbook for Getting Control of Our Emotions and Emotion-Driven Behavior,* she identifies an extensive list of common stressors that are assaulting the population (this means your employees):

- Receiving upsetting phone calls and visits from people

- Dealing with loved ones that are ill or dying

- Experiencing loneliness in their lives

- Disappointments with life

- Reaction to criticism and rejection

- Overwhelmed by deadlines (whether personal or professional)

- Medical problems (whether themselves or with loved ones)

- Physical disabilities that make their lives more challenging

- Financial concerns

- Phone calls from bill collectors

- Loved ones in precarious situations (danger, fear of losing their job, etc.)

- Separation from loved ones

- Moving (what many consider the worst experience a human could ever face)

- Rudeness of others

- Broken things at home (A/C, appliances, vehicle)

- Overcrowded or noisy environments (open concept work spaces aren't for everyone)
- Constant demands/pressures to change
- A spouse/partner/roommate that will not help out with chores at home
- Difficult coworkers
- Challenges with their children
- Loved ones away at war/military service
- Marital or relationship stress
- Bad memories of the past
- Daily hassles
- Struggles of being a single parent
- Stress
- Inconvenience
- Transportation issues (car breaks down, transit late or out of service making them late)
- Stress from significant life changes
- Not having enough time to accomplish what they want to do
- Affording medications
- Medication side effects
- Job issues in general
- Dealing with an ex
- Problems with loved ones
- Death of a child
- Divorce/separation
- Grudges

- Stuffed (held within) anger
- Traffic (worse in some places than others)
- Rude drivers (blame traffic)
- Receiving bad news
- Finding themselves in a dangerous situation (i.e., housing, financial, dealing with an ex)
- Adjusting to a new environment (home, city, office)
- Receiving bad medical news
- Loss of a pet
- Student loan debt
- Incarceration of a loved one
- Spouse loss of job
- Becoming a parent
- Losing a parent
- Increasing number of arguments with spouse or partner
- Living with someone
- Death of a close friend
- Recent birth of a child
- Pregnancy
- Experienced violence
- Subjected to sexual harassment

Now ask yourself this question... did you just breeze through that list because you were trying to move on and get to the point? What if that long, exhaustive, overwhelming list *was* the point? The way you read that list actually reflects your level of willingness to consider the impacts of these stressors on the lives of your employees.

Every single one of your employees is dealing with multiple factors on that list. It is their inescapable reality and, according to research, the less power and financial security one has, the greater the impact of each of these stressors.

Typical responses from employers at this point tend to be:

"Are you suggesting those things need to be our problem?"

"How the hell are we supposed to deal with every single personal problem facing every single employee? What a waste of time!"

So let's get clear. Employers are NOT responsible for employees' personal stress, but you do need to understand it if you want a complete picture of how your employees constitute a risk for your organization. You want to know how a person goes from employee to "powder keg?" It starts here.

HOW DO YOU SOLVE A PROBLEM? HIDE IT OF COURSE!

Most places of employment think they have solved the problem of employees' personal stress by decreeing that work life and home life shouldn't mix. (Let's ignore those instances when the employer's demands intrude on the employee's personal life, shall we?)

If an employee isn't able to keep their personal problems at home, this is usually viewed as a flaw in their character. As a result, they are relegated to the "no path to success" department. It isn't long before these employees are passed over for promotion or leadership opportunities as a form of punishment because "clearly" they couldn't "cut it".

Problem solved right?

Sure, if you consider it a solution to add disapproval, shame, secrecy and fear to a situation already under pressure. We see this as a recipe for disaster. A disaster that you are going to be left cleaning up.

It is a fact that employees are experiencing a multitude of stressors that have "nothing to do with work" that are operating at an invisible or cloaked level within the workplace. To ignore them completely is to invite trouble with your employees, and a risk few employers should take.

Let's consider some examples of real life situations where we can see how trauma, stress and irritation all interact in one's personal life that directly impacts their professional life. (Names changed due to privacy):

FROM RISING STAR TO DIMMING BULB

Phil was a long-standing, high-contributing employee within his organization and was thrilled when he was promoted to District Manager. There was clear encouragement from his employer that Phil was leadership material, and this promotion was likely only the beginning. It was excellent news for Phil's career aspirations, but it was a bit more complicated for Phil's personal life.

To begin with, Phil had to relocate to another city. This was routine practice in Phil's organization - if you wanted to advance, you moved where the company sent you. Besides, moving costs were covered. But Phil had a family of five. His wife Amy held a job she loved, and had part-time hours that allowed her to be home after school for the children. His children were very upset to leave their friends and school behind. The youngest had special needs, and the thought of getting him the support he needed in his new school district created anxiety for Amy and Phil, as advocating for additional educational supports for their son had been challenging in the past.

The move itself strained the whole family. Sure, "moving costs" were covered, but selling the house, finding another, packing their belongings…it was time consuming and stressful, and expenses soared well above anything the company was going to cover.

To make matters worse, Phil's mother in Arizona experienced significant health problems just as he began the new position. Phil was desperate to take time off work to visit her in hospital, but the timing was impossible. As a result of her deteriorating health, his mother was going to have to go into assisted living – Phil needed the extra income from this promotion more than ever and could do nothing to jeopardize that.

The level of stress associated with accepting the promotion he deeply wanted as part of his career trajectory created so much stress for Phil and his family that the promotion no longer felt like opportunity; it felt like a noose around his neck. He knew this was something he could never reveal to his employer, but his employer certainly noted something was wrong. From day one of beginning his new job, Phil was under-performing, irritable and lacked the commitment to putting in the hours to learn the position. His employer was pissed that Phil didn't seem to appreciate the opportunity for growth that had been given to him. Phil had transformed from a valuable resource to wasting his employer's time and money.

What You Don't Know CAN Hurt You

Victoria was a single parent that worked in the finance department for her organization for four years. She was a stable, dependable employee, despite the demands of single parenting. Victoria had been having problems with her teenage son for the past year and a half. He had been having issues at school that were becoming more and more serious, and Victoria's personal life was in a constant state of stress that involved repeated arguments with her rebellious son.

Victoria's car began periodically breaking down but due to her high rent costs and having a single-income household, she couldn't afford to have it looked at. This meant she was frequently relying on public transit at the last minute to get to work, which caused her to be late to work a few times per month.

Victoria's sister had been fighting cancer for six months, leaving her in and out of the hospital for chemotherapy and radiation treatments.

Victoria would often watch her sister's children, which created further conflict with her own son.

Each day was a huge struggle for Victoria as she tried to maintain an upbeat attitude despite all of the things that were happening in her personal life, but she had no room at all for any additional stress. At work she found herself increasingly overwhelmed and irritable if her boss made any extra demands on her. To her boss, Victoria seemed an unreasonable and unreliable employee and he gave her written warnings about both her lateness and attitude that "did not reflect a good team player". Victoria felt like her boss was out to get her and that it was just a matter of time before she was going to lose her job. Distressed and desperate, she shared with her co-workers, who felt great sympathy for her situation (which her manager knew nothing about), and a collective resentment began to grow among the staff for their cold-hearted manager. The entire team showed lowered productivity, increased resistance towards leadership, and unwillingness to perform any task outside their precise roles. When Victoria was dismissed, her personal story went viral when friends posted a campaign to assist in her financial crisis. The organization was a soulless "out-of-touch" monster in the eyes of the pubic. It was an unmitigated disaster.

What to take from these examples?

Stress in your employees' personal lives is very real, complicated and playing out in myriad ways in their workplace, made all the more volatile because it must remain hidden. The higher the stress, the higher the stakes. If the workplace environment is one that invalidates personal stress or emphasizes to employees that there's no place for it at work, employees are much more likely to overreact to authority, nurse grudges, generate divisive environments, and look for outlets to release the building pressure.

Situations like the ones above are happening every day for employees, yet organizations are rarely even aware that their employees are in distress until the damage is done. Millennials are screaming from the rooftops about all of their issues, there are countless other employees who are suffering in silence, seething with resentment, and moments away from lashing out at management and the organization for being insensitive, abusive, dehumanizing, sexist, and bullying... it's an alarming list of adjectives and one that has the real potential to become the next hashtag for your organization.

EXPECTATIONS AND FATAL FANTASIES – THE SET-UP FOR DISAPPOINTMENT

There is something else packed into your employees' invisible baggage that, upon first glance, doesn't look like a problem at all, but is worth noting here because it so often contributes to the creation of resentment.

Each new employee will walk through your doors filled with hopes and dreams and aspirations. These represent the optimism that the new employee has about the future and the new life they are about to begin. Optimism is great, but what can be damaging are the fantasies your employee is constructing – a narrative for themselves about what it's going to be like, and the great job they're going to do, and how much everyone is going to love and appreciate and reward them for their contribution. This is what they're "walking in the door" with. The younger or less experienced the employee, the more extreme or unrealistic these fantasies are likely to be. But *all* employees, even the most seasoned and realistic, create fantasies – no exception.

As with the external stressors employees pack in their invisible baggage, employers are not responsible for employees' fantasies, but forewarned is forearmed – it is helpful to remember they are there in the mix.

How do fantasies contribute to resentment?

It is only a matter of time, of course, before everyone's "fantasy bubble" will burst. The employee will inevitably have disappointing or frustrating interactions with people in management positions, people who have power over them, even peers, who will challenge their expectations. These interactions will inform them about the extent to which the narrative they have created for themselves is going to be realized, and every instance that invalidates their fantasy and uproots their expectations allows for a seed of resentment to be planted in its place. Employers that do not proactively plan for this predictable disappointment can expect that resentment to take root and flourish.

A resentful employee generally acts a bit differently than a stressed employee. Their behavior is often less reactive and more calculated. Resentful employees work in a manner that is unproductive, and even counterproductive, because it is their way of "acting out" their hostility about their fantasies not coming true and how they aren't getting their "due". They are the employees who create endless power battles with their superiors, will use HR to file grievances, and engage in behavior that hog-ties management because they now have to treat the hostile employee with kid gloves. They also contribute to lowered team morale and productivity, and destabilization of other staff. Needless to say, ignoring a resentful employee constitutes a significant risk for an employer.

Fortunately, there are some very simple steps that an employer can take to disrupt this cycle of expectation, disappointment and resentment that require few resources besides attention and intention. We will discuss these strategies when formulating your own pre-emptive strike plan!

CHAPTER THREE
POWER PROBLEMS -THE REAL DANGER EMERGING FROM THE TROJAN HORSE

Thus far, we've been examining the hidden "baggage" that employees bring to the workplace in the form of external stressors and unrealistic expectations. These are conditions that exist for every single employee and, for the most part, employees can usually regulate themselves in the workplace and manage the shit they bring in with them. They might express some displeasure, but the majority of them behave themselves.

The final issue we are about to discuss is the most volatile item in their invisible baggage. It has to do with their relationship to power and the extent to which they feel alienated. This particular aspect of their inner lives has the most potential to produce employees who are very dangerous to us and our organizations, especially when it interacts with personal stressors and unrealistic expectations.

THE "POWER OVER" DYNAMIC

Consider the employee who is walking in the door with a lot of stress in their life. That would be all of them, bar none! If they are unable to solve the problems generating the stress (and most cannot), this generates a heightened sense of powerlessness and alienation in their lives. The only option they have is to just keep going.

They also arrive with fantasies and unrealistic expectations that they carry with them the entire time they're working for us. These expectations, when unmet (which is pretty much all the time), produce a level of disappointment and a feeling of despair.

What do you think happens when employees who are grappling with some measure of feeling powerless due to circumstances in their lives come into an environment where their feelings of powerlessness are constantly reinforced? The very nature of an employment environment means that employers will have power over their employees, and over some of the most important aspects of their lives. Yes, we know, we give them the power to make some decisions. But that's not the kind of power we're talking about. What we're talking about is the "power over" dynamic that exists in every organization. The organizational structure requires that there is always someone who has the power over the employee.

Managers are the most common representatives of employer power that the employees encounter, and therefore the power-relationship between employee and manager is the most likely to trigger feelings of insecurity and vulnerability. It is not hard to see how this can happen. Employee vulnerability stems from the manager's power over their sense of safety such as: their financial and personal well-being (will they continue getting a paycheck each month); job security (will they continue to have a job); financial future (will they get a promotion and/or pay raise); self-confidence (will they get feedback that reinforces that they are doing a good job); and self-worth (will they be acknowledged and valued for their contribution).

To dig a little deeper into this to understand what is happening for the employee, consider the fact that the power dynamic in the workplace actually robs employees of their agency, of their sense of who they are in the world, and of their sense of security as it pertains to their financial well-being. That is a potent combination when it comes to a situation where an employee is pushed to the edge by conditions or situations, and further exacerbated by the interactions they have with management in the workplace.

Given that few employees are willing to risk their livelihood to protest whatever is being asked of them, this also leaves the door open for managers to place employees in unreasonable, unfair and sometimes inappropriate or illegal situations, since it will be on the employee to both resist the person who holds so much power over their lives *and* prove it.

Given the right circumstances, the "power over" dynamic in the workplace forces employees into a state of vulnerability that can actually become unbearable. It goes without saying that when people feel too powerless, it produces a feeling of having nothing to lose and they are much more likely to act in ways that can be very harmful, not only to themselves, but to others. They are powder kegs waiting to go off.

But the "power problem" doesn't stop there.

Organizations must understand the psychology of power and how it affects employees, and the way employees will use management as "stand ins" for their own history with disempowerment. This will provide key insight into what contributes to the worst form of employee "acting out" in their interactions with people who have power over them, and informs and enables you to formulate a pre-emptive strike that will neutralize this invisible threat in its tracks.

INTRODUCING THE "STAND IN"

What needs to be understood by executives, managers and HR professionals alike is how an employee's history/beliefs/experience of power is at the root of all their interactions in the workplace. When power is involved in any relationship, there is no such thing as a "neutral" interaction. Furthermore, because power is so loaded, each individual's history of negative experience with power will be quietly influencing the present moment – usually subconsciously. Consider the biggest and deepest issue people have in their lives – it usually involves their parents or someone who has been very powerful in their lives and has had influence over them. No, this is not parent-blaming; it's power-blaming.

Your employees' relationship with people who have power over them in the organization will always include "stand-ins" – that is, the unseen presence of influential people who have held power over them at some point in their lives. Given the significance of relationships that people have with others in their lives, starting with childhood, those relationships that represented the greatest threat to them emotionally will be the ones that become the "stand in" in the workplace. The power dynamic that is necessarily present in the workplace is what creates the "trigger" for the insertion of the "stand in". Managers, executives, HR representatives all "stand in" for the unseen influences carried in the door by employees.

Managers, in particular, are holding power at the front lines of our organizations. They are the ones employees interact with most often and who have direct control over many aspects of the employee's life. Power dynamics are at their most concentrated here for employees, and the way in which staff will interpret interactions with managers has a great deal to do with who the managers are "standing in" for in their employees' lives. An unsavvy and oblivious manager can end up generating a host of negative and unproductive reactions on the part of the employee that are often completely unrelated to the manager but, unfortunately, still their responsibility.

Let's take a look at how a "stand-in" for power manifests most commonly between an employee and their "neutral" manager who is simply unwitting and careless with their power, and yet triggers the employee, to the detriment of the organization:

THE UNMAKING OF MARK

Mark was a dedicated employee who had been with his company for five years. He was an amiable kind of guy, always one to help everyone and never taking credit for his contributions. He was the guy that everyone wanted on the team; never a "grandstander" and always the one promoting everyone else. Mark felt good when others felt good. He liked to be the "go-to guy" who everyone could count on.

Mark's easy-going nature meant that he was liked by everyone at work and he liked everyone in return, except his manager. For some reason, his manager got under his skin. Where everyone else thanked Mark and acknowledged his extra efforts, his manager just wasn't personable. He was "no nonsense", rarely gave any praise, and seemed only interested in talking to his employees when telling them what to do or what they did wrong. It wasn't a huge problem for Mark, he just didn't like the guy.

Mark's personal life took a devastating turn when his wife received a diagnosis of Stage 4 metastatic breast cancer. Her treatment was not only frightening, but expensive. Her medical bills were staggering and she could no longer work. Mark was now the only breadwinner for the family. They had a couple young children and Mark became their sole caregiver as well. Mark needed to take time off work for his wife's care and needed to be home right after work for his children. He could no longer put in the hours he previously did willingly and without compensation. Mark's manager had made a couple of passing comments about Mark no longer being a team player, but had never confronted him directly.

At the same time, Mark's mother died, leaving his widowed father who was suffering with early stage Alzheimer's without care. Mark couldn't afford a care facility and instead took his father in. Mark felt for his father, but at the same time, the relationship was complicated. He was always a difficult and demanding man. Through most of his childhood, Mark had tried to offer the emotional support to his mother that his father withheld. As his father's illness progressed in later years, he had become even more insensitive, inconsiderate and demanding. Mark's mother had spent the final years of her life catering to this thankless man, dismissing his degrading behavior as part of his illness. Now he was living with Mark and directing all that old and familiar abuse at him. Mark couldn't even confront him because he had Alzheimer's.

Two weeks after his father's arrival, Mark arrived at the office late. Frazzled and not at all his usual self, he rushed to the meeting with his manager. As usual, his manager didn't bother to look up from his computer when Mark entered, only barked that he was late while he finished an email as Mark waited. When he finally began the meeting it was short and terse – the report Mark turned in the day before was incomplete and needed to be redone and resubmitted that day, meaning Mark would have to work late.

Mark protested that the direction he had received from the manager was what he delivered in the report, but he was shut down before he completed his sentence. This manager had never been one for accepting any blame for an employee mistake, end of story. Mark stifled his inclination to protest further due to his amiable nature, but he could feel himself beginning to seethe as his manager continued to pick apart his work. Mark knew that his manager had no idea what was going on in his life, but also knew he would receive no support if he did know. If anything, it would likely put his job in jeopardy.

As Mark returned to his desk to work on the report his emotions were in turmoil. After all he had done, after all he had given for everyone at work, none of it even seemed to matter. He was never going to be good enough. He was reminded of his dismissive father, no care or concern, no feeling whatsoever, no compassion, no understanding, just someone who is self-absorbed and doesn't give a shit about him or his situation.

Mark got up and went into the kitchen and saw a text on his phone from his manager: "reminder: report EOD."

Later, Mark would say that he couldn't remember kicking the kitchen garbage can and sending it flying into the hallway. He didn't remember any of the events that followed actually, but his shocked colleagues could recount them in Technicolor detail. Mark, everyone's favorite guy, returned to his desk and began to trash it. When his manager arrived on the scene Mark began to verbally unload everything he had never been allowed to say, at full volume and laced with threats. When the manager put a hand on Mark to calm him down, Mark threw him to the ground, also knocking over the HR director who had arrived to see what was happening, who hit her head on the desk. Mark was escorted out by security and every single employee was devastated, angry and mutinous at what the organization had done to Mark. Trust with leadership was broken and at the most fundamental level, and was never fully repaired.

WHAT THE HELL IS GOING ON?

Employee blowouts that are triggered by a "stand-in" power dynamic can be among the most destructive for an organization, and typically the most difficult to spot – especially if no one is paying any attention. Mark's manager left a lot to be desired as a leader, but he also wasn't doing anything overtly harmful and he wasn't acting any differently then he always had. So what the hell happened?

It should be obvious, but if it's not, Mark's manager was a "stand in" for Mark's father. Mark had always experienced his manager the same way he experienced his father. His need to be the perfect, protective child was also playing out in the workplace as he strove to be the perfect, helpful team player that could do no right under the cold demanding male authority figure in his life. For as long as Mark could remember, he took on every responsibility, tried to help others with their needs whenever possible; he was the mediator and punching bag in his family and now, in the most stressful situation of his life, Mark was facing his childhood father at home *and* at the office. But Mark's abusive father at home could no longer be confronted due to his illness.

Meanwhile, Mark's manager had no idea any of this was happening and went about his business addressing Mark the way he always had – with what he interpreted to be a clear and professional focus on the work that needed to be done, objectives that had to be met, deadlines that existed, etc. He was completely oblivious to the change in his employee's behavior, habits and demeanor, and therefore not realizing that the tone of his voice, body language, lack of approachability and his refusal to look up from his desk was actually being received by Mark as a threat to his well-being. The manager wasn't threatening Mark, but as a "stand-in" for Mark's father, he was now the embodiment of threat.

For Mark, everything his manager said during their meeting was being interpreted through the lens of Mark's "stand in", his father. Mark saw a manager that wasn't supportive of him and didn't understand him, had never even bothered to try and was now "out to get him" the minute Mark wasn't perfect. It was unfair, dehumanizing and enraging. Mark's responses had nothing to do with the manager and everything to do with his relationship, or lack thereof, with his father.

It isn't much of a stretch to be able to see the parallels between the manager-employee dynamic and the parent-child dynamic. It's also seen in spousal relationships where, for example, one partner works and the other is a stay-at-home parent. Any time one person is in a position of power over another, the vulnerable one will always operate from a place of defense. Which is why no interaction between a manager and an employee can ever be truly neutral. Every interaction has the ability to "level" an employee, to disrupt their sense of safety in the world, to disturb their emotional equilibrium, and to confirm that they have a reason to be fearful. The more stress factors contributing to an employee's destabilization, the more loaded their relationship with the person who holds power over them.

This, in turn, leads to a dynamic where the employee is going to hear very different things than what the manager is actually saying, because the employee is now processing everything through their "threat filter". Employees become hyper-alert to how their manager is interacting with them and others. This attitude tends to spread easily, as protection from threat often induces a "herd mentality". Everything the manager says or does is subject to intense scrutiny by the employee and their coworkers, and any hint of threat from the manager, perceived or real, can send them spiraling downward. There is often no recovering from this trajectory and the costs and risks to the organization are incalculable.

All of this can be avoided if management is trained in not only simple people management skills, but in how to recognize and diffuse a power "stand-in". Truth be told, employees who are experiencing elements of internal distress and growing frustration at work actually provide very clear signals in the form of behavior changes, mood fluctuations, shifts in body language, and verbal responses that are more stressed or measured in tone.

Unfortunately, management training is woefully lacking in understanding power dynamics between management and employee, producing managers who are rarely attuned to what is going on for employees, outside the scope of work tasks, and inadvertently communicating that they don't give a shit about who they are as people. Nothing could be worse for an employee than having the perception that the person who has power over them doesn't care about them. Employees tend to operate from a place of emotion when managing stressful situations. If they are interacting with a manager who only knows how to relate to their employees around the instructional or technical aspects of the work that has to be done, it can become like the left- and right-brain trying to have a conversation with each other, speaking a language neither understands.

When you combine the following elements - external stressors with unrealistic expectations - and add in the dynamics of power over and an individual's history with power generating "stand ins", you have a recipe for an employee who is in a heightened emotional state and susceptible to reacting and overreacting to interactions taking place in the workplace, especially with management. Those reactions are exactly what set your employees in motion to behave in ways that produce the greatest risk, liability, cost and distraction for you and your organization.

CHAPTER FOUR
THE WINDOW OF TOLERANCE - MEASURING EMPLOYEE RISK

S o far we have discussed how internal stressors, unrealistic expectations, and different elements of power dynamics are interacting in the lives of your employees to push them towards behavior that constitutes risk to your business. But what good is this information if it's all going on inside our employees and can't be calculated or tracked, right?

The good news is – this risk can be measured, and we are going to show you how. But first, we need to explain an important concept known as the "window of tolerance".

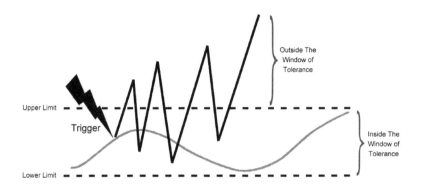

The window of tolerance is a term created by Dr. Dan Siegel that is commonly used to understand how the body and nervous system physically respond to adversity and stress, and the likely resulting behaviors. When people are inside their window of tolerance, they tend to be happy, calm, responsive, willing to engage with others, mostly neutral in their responses to things, and generally pretty rational. When they're outside or out of their window of tolerance, they tend to be aggressive and antagonistic, judgmental and confrontational, ready to pick fights, blaming others, or they might become sullen and withdrawn, unwilling to participate, feel like a victim, feel that everyone is against them, feel hopeless, and become unresponsive. All of these responses are possible when a person is out of their window of tolerance.

To make it easier to understand, think of it this way:

Imagine you are in a small, tight room about the size of a closet. The only ventilation in the room is in the form of a small window that is open, filling the closet with fresh air that makes the cramped space somehow tolerable. Now, picture the window slowly closing. Imagine the way it becomes more difficult to breathe with every inch of open window you are losing. By the time the window is almost closed, the room is stifling and you are gasping for air. You might even feel yourself panicking, kind of like getting trapped in an elevator.

The longer you are in that room struggling to breathe, the more irrational you become. You'll find you're telling yourself stories about the danger you're in, the loss that you're going to experience, that no one is there to help you, that you're completely alone with the craziness you feel inside and if you don't get out immediately, you're going to lose your mind. Ultimately what you're feeling is that your very sense of survival is being threatened.

Even if someone is in that room with you, the more they talk to you in a rational way, the more you want to attack them because you're in such a state of fear that they now become the enemy. And, as with all enemies, they must be defeated and you'll do anything to eliminate whatever is causing the extreme distress you're feeling.

This is the image that illustrates a person's window of tolerance. This is where adversity and stress clash at their worst. It's what triggers the well-known "fight or flight" reaction in an individual – meaning a person is likely to flee the situation, become confrontational, or act in a way that is detrimental to everyone around them because, for them, they feel as if they are literally fighting for their life.

In the context of a work environment, this presents some challenges. First of all, since a person's livelihood and well-being are tied to their employment, the option of "flight" is hardly an option. The power-dynamics of a workplace, however, also make confrontation a difficult option. Too often this results in employees at an impasse – stuck in a situation where they don't know how to solve their problem, and gasping for air in a tiny space as the pressure builds and builds and builds. This is the moment when they feel they have no choice but to engage in harmful behavior. Nothing about this is rational, and yet it is the reality of what is going on for the person.

Now that we see how the concept of the window of tolerance works, let's see how this operates in the workplace and how we can use it to help you identify the collective level of risk your employees currently represent to your organization.

PUTTING IT ALL TOGETHER – A SNAPSHOT OF YOUR "EMPLOYEE BEHAVIORAL THREAT RISK LANDSCAPE"

At the beginning of this book we talked about that fact that all of your employees are bringing invisible baggage packed full of elements that influence their reactions and behavior in the workplace. We've taken a look inside those bags and pulled out personal stressors, unrealistic expectations, reactions to a "power-over" environment, and personal history with power triggering the use of personal "stand-ins." All of these elements are interacting in the lives of your employees to determine where they are with respect to their window of tolerance.

How can you use this information to gain insight into the level of risk your organization is exposed to as a result of your employees? To begin with, you need an overview of the collective state of your employees.

To do this, we have developed a tool called STRAP ("Sensitivity and Tolerance Risk Assessment Program") that enables us to "take the temperature" of employees so that we have an understanding of where our employees are at in terms of the potential risk they represent. This is what we call an organization's "employee behavioral threat risk landscape".

The STRAP tool collects data through a specialized employee survey we developed that elicits pertinent information about the various stress-related factors we have identified, plus several others. Various values and weights have been assigned to each stressor, allowing us to plot where exactly an organization's employees land on the window of tolerance. Once we see where they land, we can interpret the data with an eye toward assessing the current level of risk that is present and associated with the employees.

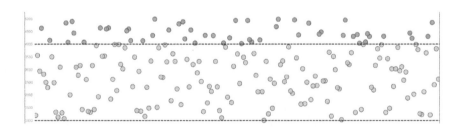

In the above chart, we see a typical cross section of a workplace. Employees within the window of tolerance (between the two dotted lines) are experiencing stress, but able to self-regulate and manage. As a result, they constitute a low risk to their employer. Employees outside the window of tolerance (those above the top dotted line) or on the verge of being pushed outside their window of tolerance (just below the top dotted line) are experiencing high stress, past the point of healthy coping, and represent high risk to the organization.

In this example, over half of the workforce are either outside the window or on the edge. This organization is in a very precarious position. It is likely they are already experiencing some internal impacts in the form of losses in productivity and profitability, and lowered morale and worker efficiency, but there is also significant risk evident that might lead to damage to the organization's external reputation. As a result, they need to act fast.

But there is a second critical factor we must examine that is the most potent of all when determining how an employee moves from within their window of tolerance to outside and therefore becomes a real and present danger to the organization. Consider the graph below:

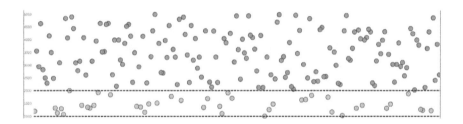

In this snapshot of the Employee Behavioral Threat Risk Landscape, we can see that this organization actually has more than 85% of their employees at the edge of their window of tolerance or out of it. This indicates that a majority of the employees now represent a significant potential threat to the organization. We can see how the window of tolerance has shrunk for most of the employees, and that suggests they are less able to manage the stress in their life and workplace; their ability to self-regulate and manage in the workplace is diminished, and the environment has become more and more intolerable.

So let's look at the workplace and ask who controls the environment. Not the employees. This is where you come in, leaders! Get ready to learn how you and your leadership team are moving this window of tolerance and directly impacting the level of threat your employees represent to your organization.

CHAPTER FIVE

HOW EMPLOYERS ARE CLOSING THE WINDOW OF TOLERANCE

Before it's possible to develop a pre-emptive strike plan, we have to look at the other side of the equation - how employees end up behaving in ways that create liabilities for our organizations. This means the spotlight now shines brightly on all of us in leadership positions, along with some of our entrenched behaviors and policies that are serving to push our employees outside their window of tolerance.

Or, to put it another way, we are going to examine some of the more common ways employers are actually "triggering" their own employees.

AN ANALYSIS OF ORGANIZATIONAL "TRIGGERS"

Remember when we warned that some of your employees have the potential to become a powder keg, just ready to blow? Well, before we discuss how you can disarm them, we have to stop you from detonating them in the first place. You may be shocked to know that some of our most common practices today are practically akin to walking up and putting a match to a fuse when it comes to the stability and well-being of our employees.

So, let's pull this apart and look at three things we've identified as the biggest culprits when it comes to our behavior and that of our organizations.

Negative employee behavior is triggered by various actions on the part of the employer, but the three top problem areas that we've identified are:

1. Interactions between management and employees

2. Executive behavior

3. The structure of the organization

Let's review them in detail.

THE MANAGEMENT TRIGGER

Without a doubt, the genesis of most employee alienation, discontent and resentment can be linked directly to their experience with their manager. If you take some time to do a little digging into your own organization, you too will find that employee/manager relations emerge consistently as your repeat offender.

We touched on this subject briefly when discussing the phenomenon of managers in the workplace standing in for other people (past or present) in the employee's life who has held power over them. Since managers are your "front-line leaders", they become the *de facto* stand in more often than not. We examined how a neutral manager who is not trained in recognizing this power interaction or trained how to deal with it (let alone care about it) can inadvertently bring a world of hurt to the organization.

Unfortunately, this is not the only way that managers trigger employees, and we all know that managers are rarely "neutral". They are people who also bring their shit to the workplace that manifests in a wide variety of ways, most often negative. But the fact that they have power over people makes their bad behavior a major problem. In today's workplace, executives who chose to turn a blind eye are likely to find that the manager's shit has traveled up the chain of command and hit their own fan!

We are going to look at some of the most destabilizing and egregious management behaviors and practices that trigger our employees and send them right out of their window of tolerance. These triggers manifest most often around careless communication and poor people management;

CARELESS COMMUNICATION

We get it. You're busy. We're all busy, and we don't always pay attention to how we communicate. Fire off an email and move on to the next task. That's the way we work, that's the way we get shit done. Problem is, those quick and careless emails can have huge consequences if they are creating problems for your employees.

The way that managers communicate (or miscommunicate) with their employees is almost always problematic, and one of the top triggers around generating resentful and threatened employees.

Here is a really basic rule: when operating in an environment of unequal power, the person with less power requires greater clarity and neutrality in order to maintain a sense of safety. This is human nature. We don't have to like it, but since we can't change it, we might as well understand it and ultimately make it work to our advantage.

Keeping this rule in mind, we also know that the majority of communications with employees come from their managers, and so it is no wonder that this is such a problematic area. Poor communication between a manager and employee will increase the stress level for an already over-stressed employee, and can create conditions that will push them out of their window of tolerance.

Let's start with a simple example: our written communications. How much unnecessary grief is generated by a carelessly written communication? Managers rely almost exclusively on email and memos to communicate with their employees. (Executives do this as well but are far less likely to email employees directly.) The biggest problem with managers' over-reliance on email really surfaces when the information being disseminated involves an important issue such as an organizational change, new policy implementations, or staffing changes. There is rarely enough clarity provided in an email and no real mechanism for employees to ask questions. If you think that having HR review the email is enough before sending, think again!

Employees will always interpret the "intent" behind the information being sent to them, and each employee will filter this important announcement through their life stressors, job fantasies, and experience of power in the workplace. Remember, you having power over your employees will always make you suspect. Once they run the email through their own internal "Employee Translation Program" you can bet the information they are left with is a more threatening, destabilizing version of the original.

POOR PEOPLE MANAGEMENT – TRIGGERING PRACTICES AND BEHAVIOR

One of the most common complaints about managers is that they suck at managing people. How many managers do you know that have been promoted past their own level of incompetence in the "people management" department? Ever notice how they remain in their positions as their employees cycle through the department like they are on an assembly line designed specifically to turn a valuable worker into a disgruntled nightmare?

When managers are hired, how are you ensuring that they are actually capable of managing people? How do you test for whether or not they have the temperament necessary to respond appropriately to their employees? How is this being evaluated?

Consider the cost of re-hiring, training, lost and diminished productivity, and lack of team efficiency. These are just the obvious drains on profit when a poor people manager is at the helm. The more disgruntled employees an organization produces, the greater the risk one of them will go public, and then the cost becomes almost incalculable.

We expect our managers to oversee departmental goals, budgets, program implementation, and track results. But precious little time (or patience) is allotted for the actual management of the people who are going to actually do this work. Managers are hired for their work experience, but rarely for their people skills. This needs to be part of their training and built into their reporting, because right now we are setting our managers up for failure. Since our managers are the ones creating the greatest level of employee alienation and discontent, we are, in turn, setting ourselves up for failure.

In our consulting work, we have identified three areas where managers fall short most often in their people management skills: over-controlling, de-humanizing, and dismissive leadership practices.

OVER-CONTROLLING PRACTICES (DON'T GET ANY IDEAS!)

Management-level leadership is plagued with "over-controllers". These are individuals who have no interest in fostering the growth or independence of their employees. They micro-manage and see their employees only as occupants of the positions they are currently hired to fill. Managers like this are guilty of restricting growth, input and knowledge, and squelching the desires of the employees under their leadership. The only upward movement they are interested in is their own.

For example, let's say you have a talented employee with a great vision for the organization and career aspirations to join the management ranks. The manager feels threatened and competitive and responds by structuring the employee's role to minimize chances of promotion. Further, the manager takes to micro-managing this employee's work in order to control and monitor them, which is experienced as smothering and frustrating to an individual with ideas and aspirations. When an employee is prevented from growing and contributing there is a real danger that a cycle of resentment will be triggered for this person. They will not only be contending with the unfairness of the present situation, but will begin to draw on their negative history of power as well – instances when they have been passed over for opportunities, when others have been given preference, and all the times when the odds have been stacked against them. Very quickly their resentment can escalate into a very serious problem that may not be possible for the employer to circumvent.

DE-HUMANIZING PRACTICES (I'M SORRY, DID YOU THINK YOUR LIFE MATTERS?)

Managers who regard their employees like they are simple departmental resources are guilty of creating a de-humanizing work environment. Every person needs to be treated equally, but they are not all the same. Age, health, physical ability and numerous other factors will impact employee performance. Managers who ignore these differences and just expect that people will "take care of their own problems and get their job done" are actively producing alienated employees who feel their employers don't care about their lives.

Childcare responsibilities provide a good example. Consider the number of times management will require employees to work longer hours (often without pay or other compensation or consideration) based on some project deadline. No consideration will be given to the onerous burden placed on the personal responsibilities of employees, such as scrambling to find childcare for these additional hours and often paying exorbitant rates for childcare overtime. This total disinterest on the part of the manager sends a clear message that if you have, or want to have, children and work, that is going to be your problem. Women are more likely to carry the burden of childcare, and any resistance or irritation they may express at being forced to take on more hours at the last minute could be viewed by management as inflexible, undependable and ultimately "a liability". Knowing this places even greater stress on the employees.

Let's not forget, when employees are expected to perform above and beyond their job duties, there is another danger lurking in the waters. If the employees perceive that this demand is a result of a failure on the part of management to properly or professionally manage the project, the collective resentment will be magnified. This holds true if there are "favored" employees involved in the project that have failed in their responsibilities and are not being held accountable, especially when the burden of their irresponsibility is placed on other employees. Since any resistance on the part of the remaining employees will usually be met with unfair or negative consequences, and since they are operating in an environment that does not consider their individual situations, the level of alienation felt by the employees will be exacerbated tenfold, and their reactions to it shouldn't be surprising.

DISMISSIVE PRACTICES (LET ME REINFORCE HOW LITTLE YOU MATTER)

Dismissive management practices are closely related to dehumanizing practices, but where dehumanizing practices stem from a regard of employees as simply "resources", dismissive practices stem from a total disregard for employees altogether. Dismissive managers are consistently disrespectful and impatient with their employees, and have no room at all for being inconvenienced by their lives.

What does this dismissive behavior look like? It's managers not taking seriously the issues that are brought to them by employees. It's not acknowledging their employees or providing feedback to them. It's being indignant or impatient with their employees if they're not pleased with something. It's not getting back to them in a timely manner. It's running out of meetings early, leaving things unfinished. It's providing incomplete information. Dismissive managers look more like a parent who silences a child with the age-old adage: "because I said so!" But this isn't a daycare center - it's a professional environment that requires managers to demonstrate a level of respect toward the people they are supervising.

POOR POWER MANAGEMENT – TRIGGERS MULTIPLIED

So far we have looked at damaging management *practices* that result from poor people management skills. Now we need to examine the most urgent and egregious areas of management *behavior* that have the potential to produce the greatest damage to the organization through employee retaliation, litigation and worse. We are talking about crazy-making, bullying, and threatening behavior.

CRAZY MAKING BEHAVIOR (MY INCOMPETENCE IS YOUR PROBLEM NOW!)

When was the last time you looked at how your managers are handling the work assigned to them?

Managers who are less than adequate in terms of managing their own workloads can be a nightmare for their employees. Managers who are inept will routinely display their inability to do their job, and it's their employees who will pay for it. These managers tend to be stressed because they cannot do their job and will take this out on their employees. Nothing frustrates and destabilizes employees more than attempting to function in a work environment of constantly changing priorities, shifting deadlines, and an atmosphere of chaos. These managers are your "Crazy Makers".

To make matters worse, these managers are rarely disciplined, (they either have the ear of upper management or are benefiting from their total disinterest). At the same time, these managers are most likely to be heavy-handed in the disciplining of their employees – who are subjected to working under conditions where the goals and conditions for success are a moving target. Managers like this create a breeding ground for employee mutiny and utter contempt for the organization's leadership.

Just a note: One of the easiest ways to identify if you have a crazy making manager in your midst is to note how frequently they throw their employees under the bus. This is a dead giveaway for a Crazy Maker.

Managers who are on top of things will always take responsibility for their area of work. A manager who is pointing the finger at their employees should be a red flag for you. Remember, an incompetent manager is equivalent to a finger pointing at you! A crazy making manager who is not held accountable triggers a domino reaction of lost confidence all the way up the chain of command. Once your employees lose faith in the leadership of their organization, there is nowhere to go but down.

BULLYING BEHAVIOR (I'LL GET YOU...ONLY 'CAUSE YOU CAN'T FIGHT BACK)

We now have to look at the prevalence of bullies in our midst. This is particularly acute in organizations that employ multiple "line" people, such as medical staff under a lead physician, nursing staff under a head nurse, or a kitchen under a head chef. In many of these environments, time is of the essence, strict compliance with protocol is required, and bullying becomes the *de facto* management style. But bullying doesn't stop there. It has been creeping into organizations that have no justification whatsoever for blind obedience and hard-nose discipline. In fact, we have actually cultivated a culture of respect for bullies in the boardroom or screaming in their hellish kitchens, not the least of which have been popularized on reality television shows.

As a result, too often there is little to no supervision of bullies inside organizations, which leaves employees feeling defenseless. Even if reports are made to Human Resources, bullying managers are rarely called to task for their behavior. As mentioned above, it is becoming more and more common for bullies to be praised and admired for their hard tactics, as a display of their strength and commitment to the organization – as leaders who do whatever is needed to get the job done.

Perhaps we leaders justify bullying because we need to believe in an inflated sense of the importance in our work? Are the balancing budgets a matter of life and death? Does preparing a meal require military precision and discipline?

41

The truth is, treating employees like mindless troops in your regiment ultimately backfires. It does not foster loyalty or willing cooperation; it creates resentment and rebellion, and promotes infantilization and petty squabbles between your employees over the few scraps of power they do have. The real results of a bullying workplace? Lowered morale, wasted productivity and resources, inefficiency, high employee turnover, and worse.

Your customers or clients also pick up on employee discontent. This is not good for profits or reputation management. Employees may not be able to strike back at their managers, but they will most certainly spew wherever an opportunity presents itself, most often in public communication forums. If anything, the only people working for you that need boot-camp style smack-down training are the bullies in your midst!

THREATENING BEHAVIOR (SHUT UP AND TAKE IT!)

We have saved the worst management behavior for last - namely, managers that engage in threatening behavior as a means of demonstrating their power. In today's workplace, employees are too commonly subjected to managers who rule by fear and routinely make demeaning, sexist, racial, ethnic, classist or homophobic remarks. Threatening managers do not limit their transgressions to words alone; they inappropriately touch or sexually harass their employees, and generally create a hostile work environment. Threatening management behavior often takes place behind closed doors or away from public areas. Employees fear retribution if they report the behavior to Human Resources. Given the employees' dependence on the organization for their financial security, they are placed in a situation where they are forced against their will to tolerate behavior that is completely unacceptable, not to mention illegal.

The actions of a threatening manager are never justifiable and have no place in a professional work environment that claims to have a commitment to the safety of their employees. Remember, these may be problematic individuals but they are the by-products of an environment that turns a blind eye to their behavior. Bullies can only exist with the permission of those in power. Leaders of an organization have to be willing to take swift action and strong public stands on behalf of those who are not in power – by the unflinching removal of threatening managers (even if they're one of your favorites).

You cannot have people working for you, (therefore representing you and your organization), who are victimizing employees. All executives need to consider how they are communicating with employees so that it's safe for them to come out of the shadows and report victimization. How are you showing that you will protect them and not the perpetrator? This isn't a Human Resources policy or training issue; this requires the proactive engagement of a leader who is constantly on the lookout for any behavior that points to a problem with a manager. Without the requisite vigilance being exercised, an organization is going to find itself in a nightmare it can't wake up from.

CHAPTER SIX
EXECUTIVE TRIGGERS – THE BIG GUNS

We've talked a lot about managers but it is time to shift the beam of the spotlight a little closer to home. It is a common perception among executives that they are exempt from culpability when it comes to negative behavior in employees. Nothing could be further from the truth. Employees are constantly on the lookout for cues, clues or hints on the direction of the organization and other pertinent things, based on what the executive says, does or communicates through internal memos, emails, or presentations. Employees also keep a close eye on executive behavior and are constantly asking themselves: Does the leadership care about us? Do they look out for us and consider *our* best interests? Are they playing favorites?

Don't forget, not only do you hold a lot of power over the lives of your employees, but you are perceived as directly benefiting from their hard work. When the organization flourishes, it is the executives who get the big bonuses, profit sharing, and perks (at least that is the common belief). So yes, you are under the microscope, and the fallout from your behavior has a domino effect down the chain that can impact every employee in your organization.

So let's take a deep breath and take a look at some of the most damaging executive- generated triggers for your employees: careless communication and power-blind practices.

CARELESS COMMUNICATION

Executives rarely communicate directly with employees and therefore their communication triggers have less to do with how they are communicating (the main problem with managers) and more to do with what executives are *not* communicating. Perhaps you will recognize some of your own practices as we explore the impacts of withholding information, uneven dissemination of information and careless handling of destabilizing information.

WITHHOLDING INFORMATION: (WHAT YOU DON'T KNOW CAN HURT YOU!)

What an organization is keeping from their employees can be just as damaging as conveying a message badly. When it comes to withholding information, no one does it better than executives, and whatever precedent you set, will be replicated by your management team.

Organizations are notorious for keeping quiet about "big picture" information or upcoming plans that have wide-ranging implications for employees, such as departmental restructuring or new organizational direction. They operate with a "code of silence" around the impending changes, not realizing that employees will always sense that something is going on. Just like management's communication, if you don't properly manage the message you are sharing with your employees, they are left to make up their own stories about what's happening. It goes without saying that they are not going to assume the best.

You set the tone for organizational communication practices. Silence that starts from the top becomes a practice at lower levels of management, where your behavior is being emulated. The resulting silence emanating from all levels of leadership only serves to generate suspicion, fear and an "us versus them" mentality among employees. Do we need to tell you that this *always* results in behavior that is unproductive and, increasingly, with actions that are harmful to the organization? Organizations with a culture of withholding information for fear of the reaction from employees will often end up suffering more blow back then if they had just been more forthright in the first place.

We realize there is no such thing as absolute transparency in an organization, nor should there be. But there is a lot of room on the playing field between "Completely Transparent" and "Code of Silence". Let's admit it, organizations are more likely to withhold information because they can't be bothered to figure out what the strategy should be for information sharing and it feels like there's never enough time. Also, there tends to be an impatience around the whole topic. Why do employees need to know in the first place? They don't need to know, right?

Wrong. They work there. They are subject to the whims of everyone who has power in the environment you create, and it is to your own peril to dismiss their urgent need to know something. Never forget, there are more of them than there are of you. It only takes one of them these days, as we've already illustrated, to create a shit storm. The organization sets itself up to face the consequences of bad behavior among employees because they are willfully depriving employees of their agency and creating an atmosphere of mistrust and disrespect. Either you control the message, or you will be at the mercy of one that takes off and has a life of its own. Just watch how far it can go when it hits social media!

UNEVEN INFORMATION DISSEMINATION (LET'S PLAY "BROKEN TELEPHONE"!)

Some executives do not struggle with withholding important information. In fact they like to share it and experience the thrill of being the one "on top" and "in the know". The problem is, executives who wield information as a form of power are often guilty of uneven information dissemination. One group of people will be told some of the information, another group may be told a slightly different story, or given a different piece of the information. Competition arises as managers and employees begin to speculate on one's status in the organization based on how much, or what, they know.

'Broken Telephone' can also ensue when a leader leaves the task of disseminating important information to someone else on their behalf. The risk is clear; their message may not be communicated accurately or in its entirely, or the messenger may mismanage the information for "power purposes". If you have something important to share – do it yourself.

Whether or not this uneven dissemination of information is intentional on the part of the executive doesn't matter - employees will consider it "differential treatment", which often results in a divisive and competitive environment that is harmful to the organization and the people in it.

CARELESS COMMUNICATION (OH WHAT? THAT LITTLE THING JUST RUINED YOUR LIFE?)

We know that decisions made in our offices are personally felt by our employees. When we have to cut hours, benefits, salaries in order cut costs, these measures have a direct impact on the livelihood and well-being of employees. It's not comfortable to think about, but when we ignore the impact on our staff, we are in peril of ignoring the reciprocal impact on our organization. Let's look at an example.

The unpleasant act of terminating or "*dehiring*" an employee is always destabilizing to the workplace. Whether your organization has a close family-like feel among staff, or relationships that are more professional in nature, termination of an employee is always a reminder that the organization has ultimate power and no one is safe.

Dehiring is a part of working life. The real problems arise when leaders do not bother to communicate properly with their remaining employees. The concern for proper, timely and standardized internal communication around termination needs to come from the top. You should not be leaving it to your managers to decide what they are going to say. This is a careless oversight of your power, and it has serious consequences.

Employees work together and form relationships. They need to know something about the dehiring of "one of their own". Leave them in the dark and they will build a collective narrative riddled with resentment and a sense of unfairness and mistrust that will not serve you or your organization. Remember, a collective narrative has wings and can be the undoing of an organization.

One final word about communication: It is important to recognize that employees are no longer operating in the 1950s. Today, information is available in an instant, and when employees can't get information from the "official" source, they will find it (or generate it) themselves. Today's workforce is much more sophisticated and emotional. They desire to be included in decisions and want information, and when executives don't strategize on what they will share and how, the resulting vacuum of information creates a disconnect between employees and leadership which inevitably creates behavioral issues in the organization that include increased gossip, diminishing performance, lack of trust, and other issues that will have long-ranging impact if not addressed.

POWER-BLIND PRACTICES

Democracy is for politics, not business. Employers are responsible for creating an equitable workspace, but that does not mean that everyone has equal power. Organizations all have some sort of top-down power structure in order to function. Those with more power have more responsibility; it's a trade-off. But that does not mean that executives can afford to turn a blind eye to the impact they have on the employees in the organization as a result of the power they hold. Failure to acknowledge your power puts you on the fast track to abusing that power, or allowing others to abuse it on your behalf.

In previous chapters we explored some of the devastating impacts that power abuse has on employees and the welfare of the organization, and here we will concentrate on power pitfalls that plague many executives: playing favorites, allowing others to abuse their power, and careless abuse of their own power.

FAVORITISM (DISTRACT, DEMORALIZE, DIVIDE AND CONQUER?)

Favoritism and preferential treatment exist in many organizations, whether or not the executives choose to admit it, and these practices create a breeding ground for alienation and resentment. Just as differential communication sows seeds of division, your preferential treatment will grow you a garden of employees who are suspicious of one another, distracted, and nurturing feelings of victimization as they obsess about whether one is gaining an unfair advantage over the other. It's a sure-fire way to lower team cohesion, productivity and morale quickly and effectively!

We have heard many executives justify *their* favoritism - do any of these explanations sound familiar? It's simply human nature to favor employees that have been with the organization for a long time; those they brought with them from the last place they worked; those who are constantly performing their roles very well deserve respect; those that support the mission and values of the organization, and do not cause problems for the management will be more appreciated by their superiors.

We don't argue that you may genuinely like some individuals over others, but when you confer the benefits of your power to some and not to others, and you base this decision not on the person's role but on the relationship you have with them, that's called favoritism and it's toxic. When it comes to executive interactions with managers and employees, any appearance of favoritism, real or perceived, is going to create a nightmare. No employee wants to feel that someone is getting something that is not available to them. Employees feel a profound sense of indignation when it comes to someone benefitting over another (unless, of course, it's them!).

And let us not forget the dynamic that begins to play out between the individual receiving the preferential treatment and those who are not. This is an extremely damaging aspect of favoritism that most executives rarely acknowledge. Those with "unfair" access to power (usually due to their relationship with executives or upper management) often enjoy fanning the flames of their peer resentment. Expect your employees to revolt in numerous ways because of the perceived injustice they see, and the resulting powerlessness they feel.

We have seen instances where employees take to the Internet with their grievances and others who go to the Board of Directors. Whatever pot they stir, they are looking for the same results: they want to make the executive pay for treating them differently and making them feel unseen. It always works. The executive ends up seeing them all right, but for all the wrong reasons.

POWER BY ASSOCIATION (THOU SHALT NOT TAKE THY BOSS'S NAME IN VAIN!)

Let's take a look at an even more damaging facet of power-blind relationships at the office that stems from favoritism. Remember, when you use your power to bestow special perks or privileges on preferred individuals – that's favoritism. But when your "favorites" start using and abusing your power for their own benefit when you are not around, that's "Power by Association". This is extremely destructive behavior. The structure of your organization requires different levels of power and responsibility to function properly. When someone starts playing fast and loose with power that is not theirs – watch out.

Let's give some common examples of how this looks in the workplace. Employees with a "special relationship" with you (and we don't mean romantic) may casually mention in the break room some news about your kids or reference a work dinner you had together. During meetings with you they may share an inside joke or a knowing look that may be silent, but is communicating volumes to the other employees in the room. This person might be sitting next to you in every meeting and you have not even noticed. You should. Everyone else is noticing who is constantly sitting next to you. As these individuals become more confident, you will see them barging in on closed-door meetings as a display of their unfettered access to you. Every time your favored team members assert themselves by emphasizing their relationship with you, they remind other employees that they are not on the inside, and that naturally alienates them.

When you are not in the room, you can bet that this employee is invoking your name or borrowing your power in order to have their needs and demands prioritized. Not only that, will be exuding an air of being untouchable as they act out their shit, and the longer they get away with it, the more intolerable they become to everyone around them. And they are your ambassadors. So much for your reputation.

Here's the hard truth: your response to this type of behavior either reinforces the alienation your employees are feeling, or makes clear to them that no one is above being held accountable for inappropriate behavior. Leaders cannot continue to have a hands-off approach to holding their executives and managers accountable for abusing power that is not theirs.

There is no question that HR departments have filing cabinets filled with complaints from employees about managers or executives who have behaved this way. The question is, how many of them have ever been fired?

Organizational leaders, we are talking to you now. You need to wake up and understand that your closest advisers, your executives and managers, are the number one culprits for triggering a crisis of confidence in your leadership and dramatic loss of trust and loyalty among your employees. No matter how much you value the people around you, recognize that there is no point at which you are not responsible for your own behavior in relation to all of your employees and for their actions taken in your name. If these petty abuses of power are not handled properly and with vigilance, your employees will stage a revolt in a way that can bring down the entire organization and you with it. It's your choice. Your actions around this will either show you to be a great leader, one who doesn't have clue or, worse, doesn't care

Careless Use Or Abuse Of Power (Power? What Power? Now Get Over Here and Be My Punching Bag)

OK, so now we have to really take the gloves off and call out leaders for their refusal to hold themselves accountable for their power.

We have seen numerous examples throughout the book of instances where executives are careless with their power. This can range from inaction (failure to supervise their managers properly or hold them accountable for their behavior), to passive refusal to recognize the impact of their power (through practicing favoritism or careless communication). There is another form of carelessness with power that we wish to mention before examining the abuse of power.

There are cases where the careless use of power over exhibited by an executive result in head-shaking resentment among employees. We are going to share an example drawn from a real life experience.

This is NOT about Elizabeth!

Elizabeth was a top-performing employee who reported directly to Harrison who held an executive position. One day, without warning, Elizabeth received an email from Frank, a middle manager from another department letting her know that she was now reporting to him. Nothing personal, Chris just needed to decrease her workload.

To say the decision came as a surprise to Elizabeth would be an understatement. Frank had a reputation for being an incompetent blow-hard among those who worked for him and an ass-kisser to anyone in power. He also has a reputation for derailing the career paths of women in the organization. The last woman he supervised reported in her exit interview with HR that Frank had advised her she would not be promoted because she was a mother. According to Frank "If employees intend to have children, they shouldn't submit themselves for higher-level jobs that require the complete commitment of the employee". It did not go unnoticed by the women in the organization that Frank was married with a stay-at-home wife who cared for their two children. None of it was taken very seriously because Frank was well liked by the executives, known as funny and an all-around good guy that just got taken the wrong way by 'people with no sense of humor'.

Elizabeth was well aware of this history as she set about educating Frank about the entire scope and breadth of her job so that she could be managed by someone who would, in effect, do nothing more than report what she said directly to Harrison.

Elizabeth was devastated by how completely Harrison had overlooked her, had not communicated with her, and she seethed under Frank's blustering arrogance. Her performance declined as she lost her confidence and drive for upward mobility. Her respect and admiration for Harrison was replaced with disdain. Not only had he overlooked her contribution, but he seemed willfully blind to Frank's contemptible behavior. Here was a manager that routinely alienated his direct reports, had engaged in harassing and illegal behavior, and was still walking the halls of the workplace – as her new manager no less!

Harrison, on the other hand, was blithely unaware of the consequences of a decision that was simply intended to make his life easier. Frank made a joke of Elizabeth's rotten attitude from time to time, but what was the big deal? This was not about Elizabeth, Harrison just needed to reduce the number of his direct reports. Only when Elizabeth hit the organization with a messy and public complaint from the Equal Employment Opportunity Commission did Harrison begin to consider that maybe some of this was about Elizabeth after all.

In the example above, Harrison's misuse of power was one of carelessness. In other abuses of executive power, they are guilty of being more deliberately punitive in nature.

Just as executives are guilty of practicing favoritism from time to time, there is also the flip side of this behavior – when an executive personally doles out employee punishment. This practice occurs in almost every organization in one form or another. Again, it is natural that an executive is not going to like every individual that works for them, but when that person is disciplined or disadvantaged professionally by actions, words, or withholding from an executive, we are moving into the very dangerous territory of retributive justice, as illustrated below:

DOING BATTLE WITH ALI

Ali was a young self-assured new hire with lots of potential in the eyes of the executive team. Nadia was a senior executive who was tasked with grooming this up-and-comer, and she shared her colleagues' high expectations for Ali.

Ali's inexperience did not temper his confidence in any way. He was excited by all the new ideas he had to offer and impatient to complete his training. Nadia felt that Ali was dismissive of her guidance and expertise, and saw Ali as entitled and ungrateful for the opportunity he had being given. Ali often experimented, loved pushing the envelope, and early on made several mistakes; none that were overly costly to the organization, but mistakes nonetheless that could have been treated as teachable moments. Instead, his behavior further irritated Nadia, who became short tempered with her underling and decided to teach him a lesson.

The lesson came in the form of "icing out" Ali. Nadia cut off Ali's access to her and ceased his training. She figured if Ali was so smart, he could just do it all on his own. As expected, Ali began to flounder. Nadia not only refused to throw him a lifeline, but found great satisfaction with Ali's struggle. She reported to the executive team that Ali was falling well short of expectations and was not the hire they thought he was. Within a short amount of time, Ali was fired for insubordination and inability to do the job. He responded by filing a wrongful termination suit that was met with great indignation by the executive team, and their united acknowledgment that Nadia had been right all along about that young up-start Ali.

There are myriad ways that executive abuse of power can play out in the workplace - from passive-aggressive to, well, aggressive-aggressive.

We've all seen executives who act more like mini-tyrants than stable leaders, and it ain't a pretty picture. Yet precious little is done to address their behavior, despite the huge cost to the organization that they claim to lead.

Executives are not immune to stress. They have personal lives and jobs that are full of pressure. They are not better equipped emotionally to deal with stress than the lowest-paid person in the organization. The only real difference is executives have more money and resources to address their problems and, more importantly, fewer people calling them on their shit.

When executives are stressed or stretched to the limit, they will act out and display behaviors similar to their employees', but somehow they have an easier time justifying *their* behavior. In fact, many executives equate their bad behavior as a badge of just how much stress they are carrying and how hard life is at the top. Ask yourself if you might consider a calm, cool and perpetually fair-minded executive as a bit of a wimp who is clearly not working as hard the rest of us frazzled, explosive leaders?

Your employees are not permitted to bring their personal problems to work. When they do, most organizations will set to work enacting policies of punishment over any real attempts to address the root of the problem. Good thing that doesn't apply to you!

CHAPTER SEVEN

ORGANIZATIONAL TRIGGERS –
THIS IS NOT A DEMOCRACY!

O rganizations have changed little in their structure over the past century. You can pretty much take a chart from one organization and drop it into any other "org chart" and they would line up. Even with the latest open office and remote work environments we've seen emerge over the past couple of decades, the classic structure endures. But the world, workforce, and rules are rapidly shifting, and if we don't update our organizational structures we will find ourselves trading-in the word "classic" for "catastrophic."

THE "TOP-DOWN" TIPPING POINT

As discussed earlier, the top-down structure of an organization allows for a distribution of power that is necessary in order to function with efficiency. We are not suggesting a collective structure for an organization. It won't work. The problem with the top-down structure is that it breeds a certain kind of acceptance that leaves leaders and executives thinking that it's "just the way it is", warranting no examination at all. After all, we need a leader, we need executives and/ or managers, we need employees - there's your structure right there; what else would it be?

What is conveniently ignored about the top-down structure of organizations is that the abuses that arise through the "power-over" structure are so often what trigger employees to behave badly, and therefore introduce some element of risk to the organization. The more layers of management embedded in an organization, the less oversight and accountability of your managers, the greater the inherent risk. That being written, we may not be able to change the fact that organizations employ top-down power structures. In fact, we don't really want to. However, it is worth examining the various triggers that arise from this reality, in order to mitigate our risk.

NOT SHARING EXECUTIVE DECISIONS (WE DON'T HAVE TO EXPLAIN OURSELVES TO YOU!)

Due to the non-democratic structure of organizations, employees are rarely involved in decisions or, if they are involved, it takes place in informal discussions with management, with little to no acknowledgment that the employees provided input into decisions. As a result, most decisions are made with little regard for the impact on employees.

Have you ever had to go through an organizational restructuring? It is an exhausting task, juggling a thousand moving parts, calculating the consequences and costs of so many interdependent decisions. You need to consider the demands of the market or clientele you are serving, and the timelines are always tight. These same challenges are present when merging or phasing out departments. Under these circumstances, the employees (the ones who actually work for you) are not going to be top priority. The problem is, you can't ignore them completely.

There is a consistent failure across organizations going through large changes when it comes to remembering their employees. The changes are often announced at the time they are rolled out, with little or no time for the employees to adapt properly. Employees can be asked to work different hours, which has a direct impact on their home lives and can create stress and issues with their families. They can also be told that they will be working in a different physical environment, such as going from having a private office or workspace to one that is shared, thereby creating environmental stressors which they had no say in and they are left with only the option to begrudgingly accept the changes or leave the organization. As most employees aren't inclined to leave the financial safety of the "nest", they will act out their displeasure in the workplace.

It gets even more fraught for employees when the decision-making process in these structures also has inconsistencies. When management is not consistent in how decisions are made, it creates an atmosphere of suspicion among employees that management isn't being fair, equitable, or honest with the decision announcements on the various initiatives that the organization is involved in.

What is important to understand is with employees, like everyone in life, change is one of the top stressors, and it's made all the more difficult when people aren't consulted or involved in the decision. A top-down power structure does not allow for everyone to be involved in decision making. Nor should it, as such an arrangement would quickly bring an organization to its knees. But this is not true of consultation. There are numerous low-cost methods to elicit feedback from employees around important organizational decisions – from surveys, to suggestion boxes, to staff or team meetings. Taking the time to gather and acknowledge employee feedback elicits a tremendous amount of buy-in, and significantly decreases employee resistance and acting out when changes are introduced.

There will be instances when employee consultation is simply not an option, but this still doesn't let our decision-makers off the hook and free to ignore the impact on employees. When staff cannot be a part of important decisions (and they usually can't), they still need to understand the decisions. This is an information age, and our employees are desperate for information, especially Millennials, in order to feel safe and secure in their workplace. Employers consistently fail to appreciate how far a little understanding can go to foster trust, security and confidence in the leadership. Take the time to invest in information sharing with your employees around how and why the decisions were made during times of organizational disruption, and it can pay off in massive dividends.

GATEKEEPERS OF INNOVATION (NOW THAT I'M AT THE TOP, MAINTAIN THE STATUS QUO!)

We have also noted that the top-down structure of an organization can lend itself to the establishment of rigid thinking – "this is the way we've always done it" or "this is the way it *has* to be done" – especially at the management level. It can be incredibly difficult for innovative thinking to travel upwards through the levels of leadership (forget any innovation coming from employees), to the detriment of the organization that would benefit from a better understanding (and new ideas) of the challenges and possibilities that exist at the level where their business or services are actually being conducted.

Not only are employees' ideas unable to rise, employees themselves are often denied opportunities for advancement because the organizational structure is all about task and functional areas. An organization can be filled with exceptional high-performing employees who are trapped by rigid job roles or rules of hierarchy, much like how the seniority system works in organizations – with the stagnant presence of "lifers" – where institutional rules dictate how employees will move throughout the organization. In the case of seniority, the length of time you have been with the organization determines how you are rewarded. With "lifers" there may be no mechanism to move out the "dead weight", thereby opening up space and opportunities for the high-performing employees.

Placing employees in an environment of roadblocks and a lifetime sentence to a cubical cell generates a workplace that is charged with stress and frustration. It's only a matter of time before the bad behavior begins.

The common denominator among employee triggers that come from top-down organizational structures may simply come down to this:

Far too often leadership and management are using the structure to give themselves permission to be lazy about their employees' well-being. Instead of looking for ways to fully maximize the contribution of their employees, they seek (whether intentionally or not) to reinforce a system that makes their lives easier, at the cost of their employees' stability. If you're still not convinced, spend a day in your Human Resources department poring through the files of employees who are no longer with your organization, and see what was underlying their reason for their departure. Odds are, the behavior of your team and the structure of the organization have been huge contributors.

SIDELINING HUMAN RESOURCES (SOFT SKILLS AND HARD BALL DON'T MIX!)

The final thing we have to consider about how organizations alienate their employees is the role of Human Resources. HR has an obligation to protect the organization they work for, while keeping in alignment with employee rights (whether legal or moral.) This line is often blurred because HR reports to senior management or the executive in charge, depending on the structure of the organization. In and of itself this is not a problem, but an issue arises when HR professionals don't have a seat at the table when it comes to the strategic vision, planning, and decision making for the organization. As a result, their own understanding of the needs of employees will never see the light of day because they are not part of the decision-making team.

Executives and management want personnel issues to disappear, while HR professionals want to have as healthy a workforce as possible. And that health is very much associated with the emotional well-being of employees. Most organizations today are making the mistake of treating their HR professionals as implementers and not policy makers. They are considered as gatekeepers, instead of visionaries who could help bridge the gap between organizational needs and goals and the environment needed for employees to feel valued, motivated and productive. What a waste to simply reduce the role of HR in our organizations to the "bad cop" when dealing with employee issues.

The tools given to HR professionals to do their work are the organization's policies and procedures. If behavioral situations arise (believe us, they do) that a current policy or procedure doesn't cover, there is always a scramble to quickly release a new policy that will address responses to that specific problem, but never address the underlying cause. Given that HR is forced to respond by resorting to policies and procedures, there will never be ability to address the alienation of employees. They have to be reactive and procedural, not proactive and investigative.

Your HR personnel carry a lot of expertise on how employees and your organization interact. Consider how HR managers are educated or trained, and their familiarity with your organization's policies and procedures. They have expertise with employment law that help them identify whether liabilities exist in the organization and, along with their health and safety lens, that's quite a resource. But remember, HR is rarely, if ever, asked to focus on ensuring the workplace is one that is proactively and preemptively identifying and addressing organizational contributions to negative employee behavior.

HR professionals may understand anecdotally that employees are dealing with extreme stress in their lives, but they do not look collectively at employees as a category of risk. They do not look at the equation of stress and interactions with managers and executives as triggers towards negative behavior. As such, HR remains focused on responding to individual bad behavior and will never considering how to improve the overall emotional health of the workforce, even though this is the very thing that will have the greatest impact on reducing the liability, risk, cost, and distraction for the organization, brought about by employees.

THE START-UP SYNDROME (WE'RE JUST ONE BIG DYSFUNCTIONAL FAMILY!)

For the most part, we have been talking about organizations that have a fair number of employees, but we would be remiss in not talking about a particular characteristic of small organizations and start-ups that is particularly problematic for employees. Start-ups are guilty of creating the same triggering behaviors that we have been covering thus far, but there is a particular toxic dynamic that can manifest as a result of top-down structures in these smaller and younger organizations that bears mentioning.

Start-ups (and many family-owned businesses) are far more likely to have a less experienced leader at the helm who is learning on the job, and is likely not as skilled in growing an organization unless they have experience with founding multiple organizations. Regardless, small organizations mean that power is more centrally concentrated, and if that leader is the visionary or founder, there will be issues of over-controlling through power that can quickly alienate employees.

Smaller organizations also tend to have a small group of lower-level leaders who will have surrounded the founder, usually from the inception of the organization – often enjoying the energy of quick problem solving, building a new business, and sharing power and roles among themselves more fluidly than in a typical work environment. This can, however, lend itself to the creation of a tight group with relationships that feel more familial than professional in nature. This can result in a group of managers who are competing for the attention of the leader or who are resistant to being held accountable. In effect, the office environment begins to resemble a parent/child relationship, where the founder is the parent and the leaders are busily engaged with parental approval and sibling rivalry. Yikes!

As a small organization like this grows into a larger one, the family will become even more dysfunctional, as new employees will impact the dynamic and power will begin to concentrate with each family member. Founders many find themselves with executives and managers who are setting up their own families, as they foster their own team's loyalty to themselves rather than to the leader of the organization or its mission. Meanwhile, employees outside this circle will be observing these unprofessional dynamics, lowering their confidence and trust in the leadership. When they are negatively caught in power tussles from the top, resentment flourishes, as does the acute sense of alienation as an outsider.

Let us not forget that in a workplace such at this, employees will never feel safe to report anything to management, because they will never know what the relationships truly are between people in management and, more importantly, whether the leader will hold anyone in management accountable. These environments are cesspools filled with drama with all real power concentrated at the top and with an infantilized leadership team. The only way these organizations ever change and provide any hope for the employees is if "adults" are brought in to run the organization. For this to happen would mean a wholesale cleaning out of everyone in a position of power, and that rarely ever happens.

Before we move forward, let's recap the way organizational triggers interact in the work place to exacerbate employee stress and foster alienation and resentment. Consider that you have an environment where the power-over dynamic exists, which means that a large group of people have limited to no power over one of the most important aspects of their lives. This structure lends itself to some particularly destructive employee triggers, such as: unaccountable management acting in ways that are insensitive or threatening; executives behaving in ways that reinforce that employees are not valued as much as others in the organization, and abusing their power; the organization not being inclusive or participatory; limiting the Human Resources role to policy enforcement and not advocacy; no programs in place to bolster and facilitate the emotional well-being of employees; and a generally dismissive attitude toward employees pervading the workplace.

Put any of these together, (or ALL for some organizations) and you have an environment that is a breeding ground for employee dissension, discontent, disillusionment, distress and distraction – all working together to send your employees right out of their window of tolerance. If there is no outlet for employees to deal with this building pressure, it is going to turn on you and your organization. It's not a question of whether it will happen, only a matter of when.

CHAPTER EIGHT
FANNING THE FLAMES -
RESPONDING TO TRIGGERED
EMPLOYEES

There is one final element of organizational behavior worth mentioning and that is the way corporations respond to problematic behavior in the workplace – both for our employees (Cycle of Punishment) and for our management/executives (Cycle of Pointlessness).

These are not triggers *per se,* since we are not at the point of responding to bad behavior, but it is safe to say that our typical organizational procedures for managing triggered employees often act as incendiaries that fan the flames of employee alienation, rather than quenching the fires of resentment.

THE CYCLE OF PUNISHMENT - DEALING WITH TRIGGERED EMPLOYEES

When it comes to dealing with employee behavior, organizations are still in the era of being responsive rather than being proactive. It will only be at the point where a problem with an employee surfaces that the manager or executive will take note. The manager or executive almost never spend any time in advance addressing the early indications that a problem is taking root, nor do they identify previous patterns of negative employee behavior in a department or across the organization. It is always a matter of dealing with the individual once they can no longer be ignored.

Consider that management and HR responses to negative behavior among employees are often short-sighted and lack any deep thinking or conversations with the employee about why they are behaving the way they are (because there are no resources available or structures in place that would assist them to have such conversations). Add to this the common organizational culture of dismissing problematic employees with simplistic labels such as "lazy", "not team players", "troublesome" or "selfish". These are all ways of placing the blame on the flawed character of the employee who does not merit the time or resources for a deeper exploration of what may be going on. It also betrays the organization's contempt for employees who have anything going on in their lives that might interfere with their job performance, and their willful blindness around triggers that may be coming from the organization and leadership team.

When it comes to dealing with the behavior, most organizations engage with their employees in a punitive way. Almost all organizations respond in similar ways, including:

- Management and HR meeting with the employee(s) to scold them and instruct them to stop misbehaving.

- After several verbal discussions, HR will then go to the Policies and Procedures Handbook and start "writing up" the employee for their actions.

- If the employee is still acting out, then the infamous "Performance Improvement Plan" aka "PIP" gets rolled out. (When an employee is put on a PIP, that is a red flag moment indicating that HR is setting a path to dehire the employee). Many of these PIPs have obligations and targets that even the most steadfast employee would have a hard time meeting.

- Once the PIP timeline has been exceeded, organizations will either have the "last chance meeting" with the employee or they will simply terminate them.

This is a routine exercise for most organizations. Human Resources and management see the bad behavior as an irritation, and often chalk it up to being a bad hire, and then once they eliminate the bad hire, they proceed to bring in another bad hire. This model of addressing employee behavior has failed miserably, and yet organizations continue to use this model of employee "engagement" day after day. Employees are keenly aware that this is a typical organizational response to negative behavior, because they see and are affected by the after effects of the "corrective action".

It should be noted that the punitive nature of the corrective action used by organizations sets up a situation where employees aren't given an opportunity to really talk about what's going on for them, nor are conditions created where they feel safe in doing so. This is not built into the cycle at any point in time. This is unfortunate, because employees tend to talk a lot during this process, and if there are no productive channels for them to vent and process, you can bet all that negative energy is headed straight for your other employees, like a heat-seeking missile, as they begin to build their case and generate support and buy-in from their peers.

Typical employee behavior during the corrective action process (aka Cycle of Punishment) will include:

- Continuing erosion of the relationship with their manager and increasingly open contempt for those in authority.

- Increased aggression or passive-aggressiveness.

- Gossiping, complaining, gaining sympathy from and pleading their case with peers or, in other words, getting the tribe to side with them over management.

- Actively promoting a workplace where other employees are made to feel that they too are unsafe, misunderstood and victimized by the organization.

- Publically sharing (and posting) about their experience as a form of retaliation.

A high-performing organization can quickly devolve and produce a culture of non-performance if the issues employees are facing are not addressed in a way that can be productive for the employee which, by extension, means productive (not to mention safer) for the organization.

It is important to state once again that corrective action almost never results in positive modified behavior. It more likely produces an increase in resentment and bad behavior, further alienation of employees, and a more toxic work environment – all leading to greater incentive for and probability of employee retaliation. So why do we keep doing it?

CYCLE OF POINTLESSNESS – ADDRESS ORGA-NIZATIONAL OR LEADERSHIP PROBLEMS

There comes a time in an organization's existence that the strategy of punishing and terminating individual employees becomes too expensive and the problem too widespread to continue without addressing the possibility that the problem is originating within the ranks of leadership or the organizational structure. So what is the typical response? Yet another eye-rolling exercise in pretending we're dealing with the program. It often looks something like this:

- Bringing in the requisite management and organizational development consultants.

- Surveying employees about their discontent.

- Counseling management and Boards.

- Implementing some public changes based on organizational audit findings such as restructuring the organization, redefining employee roles, promoting a few "deserving" people or firing a problematic manager.

The intent behind all these actions is to quiet things down long enough for everyone to get back to work. Until it all happens again. In most cases, the management of the organization that was facing upheaval may have moved on to other higher-paying, higher-profile positions, and the unsuspecting incoming leader will be left with the same problems and no way to solve them. If the leadership remains in place, it's back to business as usual and pretending nothing ever happened. It's a vicious and unending cycle.

So what do we do when the restructuring or removal of people, or increases in cursory benefits doesn't produce the desired results? Management will bring in more consultants to do morale- and team-building exercises. Typically, employee morale has deteriorated to an all-time low at this point in the cycle, and outsiders coming in to tell them how to "play nice" with other people in the organizational sandbox is often the last straw. The organization is now packed with employees who have no confidence that the leadership can deliver real change, and they are lacking an outlet for effective communication inside their workplace. Is it any wonder that employees find a public outlet for their frustration that conveniently reinforces the Cycle of Punishment that the employer set in motion in the first place?

CYCLE OF PASSIVITY – GETTING BEYOND "IT'S NOT PERSONAL, IT'S BUSINESS"

Does it sound like we are blaming you personally? We aren't. We don't think this is your fault actually, but it *is* your responsibility. Today's successful executive is most often a high performer who is realistic about the often times ruthless environment they work in. "It's not personal, it's business" is a tough truth that has long guided our decisions and excused us from having to spend too much time looking out for the "little guy".

Who has time for "personal" - not to mention, who has training for "personal"? Rare is the executive or leader who was schooled in human behavior, outside of a few paragraphs in a college Human Resources textbook. Executives and managers are not equipped to deal with the reality and complexity of employees' lives. It's easy to interact with an employee around the clear guidelines of their job. Start venturing into the grey areas of someone's personal life, and visions of liability began to swim before our eyes.

And really, who cares about "personal"? In the cutthroat world of business, we are not encouraged to care. Quite the opposite. There is much more likely to be a deep impatience and disdain for personal, since work is no place for employees to bring their shit. The non-profit sector can at least pat themselves on the back for being a bit more sensitive to their employees, but these organizations are often rife with internal drama involving the leadership and management, so they aren't much better. And when the funding dries up, all sensitivity goes out the window as cuts are made and already underpaid and overworked employees are sent out to pasture. But at least they get a smile and thanks for being such a dedicated worker.

Now, the most important question: who has the money for "personal"? In the private sector, all executive accountability is to the shareholders and increasing their profit. This is our job. This is how our performance is evaluated and how our future success (or failure) will be determined. From our MBA classrooms to the executive boardroom, we are bombarded with the message that our only concern should be the bottom line. Employees are considered tools that are used to accomplish organizational goals. Computers are considered resources, and so too are the skills necessary to operate those computers. There is no incentive to view employees in any other way.

In the non-profit sector, leadership is under the microscope for every penny that goes into admin costs. Donors want their dollars to go to programs, not employee benefits or a new desk! So of course employee wellbeing is given short shrift. But this just can't serve as our excuse for inaction and inattention any longer. Even as more and more social media horror stories come to light, and more and more evidence is emerging that mishandling of employees constitute the fastest growing risk to organizations in terms of productivity, internal costs, public reputation and profits, organizations continue to ignore the liability that employees represent. Who has the money for "personal"? If you think you don't, just think how much you'll need when it comes time for the "personal" to become very public and costly? Where's the line item in your closely watched budget for that?

Do yourself a favor and ask what your disgruntled employees are really costing your organization. And, don't believe the excuses that this is just too hard to measure and quantify - you simply have to be creative about it and tie it to liability, risk, cost, and distraction. How much bad press do you need to have? How many lawsuits do you need to settle? How much damage control do you have to do over lost goodwill? How many sales will you have to lose? What's your employee turnover rate? How much are you spending on hiring and training? Rather than always looking at the profitability of the organization, why don't you spend some time looking at the real costs incurred? Add it up - it's really simple. If your organization doesn't put the "human" back in "Human Resources", one of your employees is going to put the "human" back in "human rights complaint", and how much do you think that's going to cost you?

So let's break this cycle of punishment, pointlessness and passivity, and get busy formulating a pre-emptive strike that will level the malevolent threat simmering at the heart of your organization.

CHAPTER NINE

PREPARING YOUR PRE-EMPTIVE STRIKE PLAN

As we prepare to develop your pre-emptive strike plan, allow us to summarize the key concepts we have covered in the book thus far:

- There are things going on in the lives of our employees that create the conditions necessary to produce risk for our organizations.

- Employees are naturally resistant to people who have power over them, which can result in negative behavior that creates risks for us.

- Employees will introduce emotional dynamics into the workplace that will have a detrimental effect on our organizations.

- Managers are behaving toward their employees in ways that are triggering negative reactions that produce risk.

- Our own behavior as leaders in our organizations is sending messages to our employees that we are tone deaf and don't care about them.

- We unwittingly create conditions and situations that alienate our employees.

- Powerlessness and alienation are the greatest contributors to employees acting in ways to harm our organizations.

All these interactions are not unlike a mathematical equation (nothing like math to impress at executive levels right?). There are a number of moving parts that generate the organization's risk level associated with employee behavior. Our equation is inspired by one that you might recognize:

$E=mc^2$

We're equating our situation with Einstein's greatest equation, one that has to do with kinetic energy? Ridiculous, right? Well, not so fast! Our equation has to do with energy and explosions too, but we're going to change it up just a bit.

Here's what our equation looks like:

$(A \times B \times C \times D) \times [(F \times G \times H \times I) \times J] = E$

Here are the factors on the left side of the equation:

What the employee contributes to the formula:

A) External stressors

B) Unrealistic expectations

C) Power-over dynamic

D) Stand-ins

Here's the right side of the equation:

What the employer contributes to the formula:

F) Management triggers

G) Executive triggers

H) Organizational structure triggers

I) Human Resources triggers

J) Punitive responses - post trigger

Here comes "E"...

The EXPLOSION!

Kinetic energy can be very dangerous, and it all has to do with things being set in motion. In our situations, we have employees that have what we shall call "pre-existing conditions" packed into their Trojan horses. Create some force against them, (e.g., managerial triggers), and what we get is a powder keg that goes off at the site of impact, with all the collateral damage that results.

This is where a pre-emptive strike plan can yield significant benefits by neutralizing the behavioral threats that have infiltrated our organizations. And this is where our planning begins.

KEEPING THAT WINDOW OF TOLERANCE OPEN

Remember the graphs we showed you, based on our STRAP tool, where we illustrated the extent to which employees of one organization were outside of their window of tolerance? Let's return to this again as a way of discussing the desired outcome of your pre-emptive strike plan.

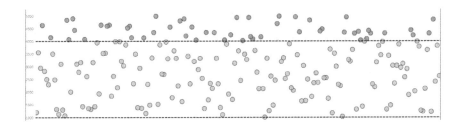

The first chart represents a collective snapshot of where your employees land on the window of tolerance – are they inside the window and able to manage their stress and regulate their behavior, making them low risk, or are they outside or nearing the upper limit of the window of tolerance, resulting in a high-risk scenario?

Think of this graph as a representation of the left side of our mathematical equation.

What the employee contributes to the organizational risk formula:

A) External stressors

B) Unrealistic expectations

C) Power-over dynamic

D) Stand-ins

Now for the second graph that shows the employees' position with a smaller window of tolerance, resulting in a much higher level of employee risk:

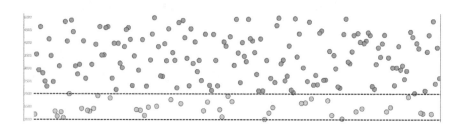

We can see the additional impact of the factors on the right side of our mathematical equation – as these are the influences that reduce or close the window of tolerance:

What the employer contributes to the formula:

F) Management triggers

G) Executive triggers

H) Organizational structure triggers

I) Human Resources triggers

J) Punitive responses - post trigger

So here is the good news:

For all of you who have been worrying that we are asking you to manage your employees' personal stress or psychological reactions to power – fear no more! Of course not. You are not responsible for the factors on the left side of the equation, but it sure helps to know that they are there.

But you *can* manipulate the factors on the right side of the equation – in fact they are completely your responsibility! We are going to show you exactly how to keep the window of tolerance open as long as possible for your employees, so you can stop slamming it shut and suffocating the people who are working for you – ratcheting up the pressure until they will take desperate action just to be able to breathe again.

This will be the crux of your pre-emptive strike plan, because this what you can actually control. Like any good operation, we will need a detailed plan, and clear roles and responsibilities. We will need to train, and most importantly, we are going to need steadfast leaders with a clear vision.

Let's get started:

MANAGEMENT TRAINING IN COMMUNICATION AND IMPACT OF POWER

Given that the employee/manager relationship plays such a critical role in stabilizing (or destabilizing) an employee, and managers are the front-line representatives of organizational leadership and power, we turn our attention here first.

It's time to put our managers through basic training for communication. They are the organization's eyes and ears on the ground. They are best positioned to spot any potential employee problem long before it spins out of control or escalates to the point of costing your organization time, money, reputation…you know the drill.

This means managers need to know their employees. They need to have a basic understanding of what's going on in their lives so that they can be aware of subtle (or not so subtle) changes in behaviors of the employee. They need to have some level of respect from their employees, as well as employee confidence in their leadership. They need to make sure their employees feel safe in the environment and that action will be taken to address the needs they feel safe enough to communicate.

Finally, managers need to know why they are being trained. They need to understand how employees constitute a threat to the organization, and their own contribution to escalating that threat and increasing organizational risk.

Remember, we are not just making nice suggestions for people to feel better. We are putting together a strategic strike plan. Management training and support will require a few things:

1. Training on how to communicate with employees.

2. Providing managers with clear communication goals, deliverables and resources.

3. Addressing and mitigating abuse of power (perceived or real).

The following is a list of suggestions for how this can be accomplished:

- Managers will need communication training. If you tell them to get to know their employees, you can bet that most of them will consider the job done after "how was your weekend?". And a handful of managers will mistake themselves for counselors, making them liable for asking inappropriate or prying questions. Their training should include "indirect communication" that includes the non-verbal messages they are sending to their employees, as well as how to read the obvious stress signals that employees give off. There are clear guidelines and trainings available for effective communication for management. This may be one of the best investments you could make.

- Training is not enough. Work with your managers to develop formal practices for fostering good communication. One possibility would be scheduled check-ins with their employees with clear, standardized questions that make it possible for employees to give feedback. What is important is that there is clear organizational value placed on facilitating employee feedback and communication, and you have equipped your managers to do so.

- Build reporting goals and deliverables into your manager's job around employee communication so that s/he can also track a sense of achievement and success, as well as flagging areas of challenges that are arising with the people they report to.

- As the people holding power at the frontlines, managers will require ongoing support. They should have someone, outside of their own managers, who they can consult for advice when problems arise or are identified when communicating with their employees.

- Provide your managers with information about resources that are available for employees that are struggling (i.e., do you have an Employee Assistance Program, HR counseling, employee support groups; do you supply taxi vouchers – this is an area where you can get creative. Not only does this foster an environment of care where a little action goes a long way, but it also means your managers will be much less uncomfortable when personal situations arise because they will have something they can actually do in response.

- Provide training programs that educate managers about the differences in the people who make up their workforce. Gone are the days when employees are treated as being all the same. Today's workforce is made up of everyone from Millennials all the way up to seasoned veterans nearing the end of their career, or older employees who are still required to work because of financial demands. Each age group must be handled differently, and it is important for managers to understand that differences exist, what those differences are, and what to do about them.

- Managers need training in proper written communication practices that takes into account how to share sensitive or potentially destabilizing information, as well as the clarity and neutrality that are required when operating in an environment with uneven power dynamics.

- Power must be addressed. Explicit conversations must be held among the leadership about power in a top-down environment and how it typically impacts or triggers employees. There should be an understanding of the role of "power-over" dynamics and stand-ins for those that hold power. There must be explicit understanding around how managers are responsible and accountable for the power they hold and how careless use of their power equates to abuse of that power. There must be clear training and guidelines around consent. We suggest formal training in this area for managers.

- Managers in private offices sets up a dynamic that communicates to employees that it is not an open, collaborative and accessible environment. Manager integration into the daily lives and space of employees serves to strengthen the relationships between them, provided the manager has been educated on how their behavior has an impact on employees.

These are a handful of suggestions of how managers can be trained on the front lines of your organization to spot potential problems within the ranks but, more importantly, create a stabilizing and safe environment that fosters a sense of loyalty and productivity in your employees, and results in less risk to the organization.

Before we turn to some executive and organizational strategies let's return, one last time, to the story of Mark. We remember the impact his blundering manager had when he interacted with Mark – oblivious to the fact that Mark was staggering under mounting stress in his personal life and that his manager was currently "standing-in" for Mark's unreasonable, demanding and abusive father.

RE-IMAGINING MARK

Let's imagine how different this scenario might have been had the manager brought Mark into his office the morning he was late and, instead of barking about his lateness, he actually looked up and simply asked how Mark was doing. Imagine Mark, appreciative that someone even noticed he was having a hard time, breaking his barely contained silence to share what was going on - even getting emotional. In this scenario, Mark's manager didn't get uncomfortable and make Mark feel ashamed or more vulnerable than he already was; he acknowledged Mark's stress and suggested various forms of support (from the list provided by the organization) that might truly benefit him, such as an online support group for family members of cancer patients, the number for the company Employment Assistance Program that would connect Mark with Alzheimer's support organizations in the community, or perhaps an extension on the report deadline. He may then have offered Mark the use of his office so he could collect himself for a little bit, before returning to his workday when he was feeling settled. Mark would instantly begin to feel safer and calmer, and feel a deep sense of gratitude and respect for his manager. The Mark in this story would not go out and trash the kitchen, but he might go back and talk to his co-workers. And you can imagine the information he shares with them would go a long way toward increasing their own respect and trust in this manager.

REAL LEADERS LEAD THE CHARGE – THE ROLE OF EXECUTIVES

We have talked a lot about the role of managers because they are a huge component of triggering dangerous employee behavior, and therefore have to be incorporated into any solution that has a hope of being effective. But any real and lasting change, any effective solution, is going to have to come from the top. Not that this will come as any surprise to you if you are an executive.

Leaders who are cognizant of the risk employees pose will never leave their management team to run the organization, lest the misbehavior of managers creates the downfall of the organization. Managers are certainly responsible for the implementation of many important elements that keep our businesses healthy but never the leadership of the organization (other than to reinforce the organizational culture and goals).

Leaders that have a complete hands-off approach and let their managers run the show are asking for disaster. Managers do not have a complete picture of all of the internal and external needs and mandates of the organization, so giving them the keys to the Ferrari when they don't have their driver's license is not a wise choice. So now we are going to look at how you can take the wheel and steer your organization away from an employee-related disaster.

First, we are going to look at the importance of setting systems in place that hold managers and executives accountable for their destabilizing and negative behavior.

DIFFUSING EXECUTIVE AND ORGANIZATIONAL TRIGGERS

In this section we will be looking at pre-emptive actions that can be employed to address both executive and organizational triggers. This is due to the high level of overlap between these two areas. Executives, after all, are the ones able to determine or change organizational practices and policies.

As discussed earlier in the book, the lack of accountability that exists for executives (and, to a lesser extent, management) around abuse of power, and negative and harmful behavior in the workplace is a highly contentious trigger for employees. Not only does it erode faith in the leadership, and thus loyalty to the organization, but it diminishes morale and productivity, fosters resentment, and triggers a deep desire within employees to see this unfairness punished. This should be a waving red flag for any organization.

When manager and executive behavior is called to task, there needs to be real commitment to change. No more turning a blind eye, bogus internal investigations, or cronyism. We should not be exempt from accountability. Nothing is more demoralizing, destabilizing, and ultimately toxic, for an organization.

The following are some practical suggestions for how you might address this toxic trigger in your organization:

- There needs to be a culture of acknowledging that the behavior of managers, executives and the organization has an impact on how employees respond in the workplace, and this, in turn, has a negative impact on the bottom line.

- There should be regular scheduled performance reviews for managers. These should include an aspect of peer review from other managers and employees. There should be a focus on employee supervision/communication performance, as well as the ability to manage their departmental responsibilities.

- Every organization, without exception, needs a process in place for managing complaints against superiors that is transparent, managed by a non-biased party, and not punitive. The more employees feel safe addressing the problematic behavior of their manager, the quicker you can get to the root of any problems (either with management or the employee) before they spread. Practices such as these radically reduce the potential for risk in the form of employee retaliation against the organization.

- That being written, an organization must have a commitment to investigating leadership properly, with clear policies in place for addressing whatever is uncovered. There should never be an assumption that the manager is to be believed over an employee, or that the burden of proof is on the employee to prove it. This is determined by the investigation.

- Your organization needs official zero-tolerance policies that address management and executive bullying and harassment.

- When negative employee behavior does require an organizational response, you need a process that goes beyond "The Cycle of Punishment". This should include an analysis of how the organization is contributing to the employee's distress or if the distress is emanating from other stressors in their life. It should never be a given that an employee is just a bad character. They just might be a "canary in a coal mine", and overtly signaling a change that needs to be made before it is too late.

- It is critical to take a hard look at past situations that have spun out of control and deconstruct what happened to identify where management or the organization contributed to the situation, how it was resolved, what the organizational impact was, and what might be put in place going forward that could move the organization in a direction that would preemptively deal with situations before they happen. There needs to be money, time and deliverables assigned to this activity.

- Give HR a seat at the table when developing all strategies for mitigating employee risk.

EXECUTIVE BEHAVIOR AND POWER MANAGEMENT

Now we want to ask you, executives, to consider some changes you could make to your own behavior that could go a long way in diffusing employee risk.

ARE YOU PAYING ATTENTION?

When was the last time you walked around your office? Not to the coffee machine or restroom, but where you walked into each of your employees' workspaces and asked them how everything is going? They won't tell you the truth, but you'll signal to them that you know they're there. It also gives you a chance to take the temperature of the environment. Are you picking up on any clues or cues your employees are giving? Are you sensing dissension within the ranks? Are you seeing non-verbal communications being exchanged? Are you seeing employees huddled together?

The signs are all there, but if you're hunkered down in that bunker of an office you work in, you're going to miss everything that is staring you right in the face. And it's just a matter of time before the bomb goes off in your office, figuratively or literally. Obviously, this is something your managers should be doing as well.

FACING THE REALITY OF THE "OTHER" ENEMY WITHIN

You need to take an unflinching look at the people who are surrounding you as the leader. If your power is being bandied about by them, then you have to be willing to take them to task, including disciplining or terminating them, because their behavior is triggering other employees. If you aren't willing to do that, you are sending a message to your employees that you don't care, and you are empowering the people around you to bring you down.

These people may be your most trusted lieutenants, or you may feel you can't run your organization without them. But, as is always the case where there is power, people will act in their own self interest. Go ahead, just try them. Push back on them and see how they behave. They'll show you every time - when push comes to shove, they may snap back at you, but it's better than your other employees taking a giant bite out of your ass.

TAKE TIME FOR GOOD COMMUNICATION

Face it, the busier you are, the less you're paying attention to how you're communicating. The level of miscommunication is going to increase, as is your irritation that people aren't understanding what you want from them.

It's like a vicious cycle: the more responsibilities you have, the less time you have. The more people need to hear from you, the less likely you'll want to talk to them. But you are the only one who can stop this cycle. Like it or not, your communication with the 'troops' is one of the most important things in ensuring trust in your leadership and a stable environment. Make careless communication a habit and you may find mutiny aboard your ship. You know how mutiny ends, don't you? The crew doesn't leave, they pitch the captain overboard.

BUILDING LEADERSHIP

Ultimately, a great leader is not just one who is accountable and responsible with their power, it is someone who is not afraid to share their power. The strongest organizations are run by leaders who are busy fostering leadership in everyone around them, and promoting this approach down the ranks to the newest hire coming on board.

This must be mirrored in the organization's structure, as well with the policies and practices that foster employee productivity, success and professional growth. Because ultimately this is the point. We have talked a lot about protecting ourselves from the harm that can be done by employees, but we have not forgotten that we are talking about the people who make our organization or business actually run. They are our human resources and it is worth our effort and attention to be sure they are humming along as productively as possible.

The following are some examples of policies and practices that enhance employee productivity and promote success and growth:

- Decrease the number of meetings being held. Meetings are a huge stressor for employees, not only in terms of the amount of time it drains from the productivity of employees, but in the ways in which negative dynamics have a way of showing up at meetings. Managerial preferences for certain employees are often on display in meetings. Employees who are trying to prove themselves to management will often dominate the room and ingratiate themselves to the leadership, who are clueless to the fact that they don't pull their weight with the team. You can bet the team sitting in the meeting knows though. Be sure that if a meeting must be held, only bring the people into the room that must be there.

- Create opportunities for employees to explore passions that fulfill them, as opposed to academic-only programs designed solely for the purpose of higher education. If there are funds set aside for professional development, there is no need to overly control exactly how these are used. A creative writing course can be just as beneficial as an "E-blasts for Communication" certificate.

- Can we just ditch the staff retreats already? They usually just end up further emphasizing the difference and discomfort between management and employees. Employees are required to attend, but no one bothers to get their buy-in. Forced team-participation events do not make for stronger organizations; they make for a greater sense of 'us and them'. Frequent meaningful conversations between management and employees will have a more lasting effect than a summer BBQ or bowling event.

THROWING OPEN THE WINDOW OF TOLERANCE

All of the strategies, behavioral changes, and organizational adjustments listed above deal with addressing the organizational contributions to employee risk – that is, all of those factors found on the right side of our mathematical equation that serve to narrow or close the window of tolerance and squeeze our employees into a state of higher stress and negative behavior.

We have one more secret tool for you that could be a game changer.

What if we told you that there is a way to do more than just keep your employees where they are relative to their window of tolerance?

What if you could create a bigger window of tolerance for each employee?

What if you could change your employee behavioral threat risk landscape from this:

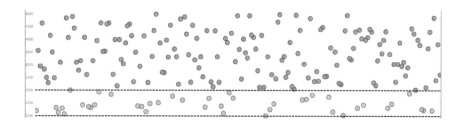

To this:

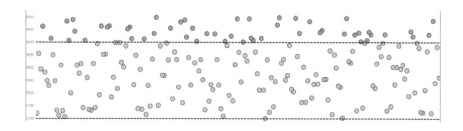

In this scenario, almost all of your employees now constitute low risk. Although their lives, stressors, and history with power remain same, they are *less* stressed.

How?

By making some adjustments to your workplace, and the policies and programs that target employee stress. Employers should stop wasting time wishing, pretending, or demanding that employees leave their personal problems at home, and look instead to small, cost-efficient changes that can be made in the workplace to reduce their levels of stress – offering big returns on relatively small investments.

The following are examples of how this can be done through the adjustment or introduction of policies and resources that target employee wellbeing.

EMPLOYEE WORK POLICIES

- Mandatory work breaks during the day can reduce the level of stress employees are feeling, and also make clear to them that working all the time is not part of the culture of the organization; that balance is critical to the health and wellbeing of the employee and the organization. Insist that employees take their breaks. This also includes respecting the break they take that starts at the end of the workday and begins the next morning. Which means do not send work emails to them in the middle of the night.

- Lose the watch! An obsessive focus on strict starting times is never matched with vigilance to be sure your staff leave on time. Deal with chronically late and underperforming employees as individuals, and leave the rest of them to act like the adults they are. Either that, or insist on equal perfect punctuality with all members of management and executives. Stop with the petty double standards. It just rubs salt in the wound of the power differential, and serves little purpose.

- Longer term maternity leave programs recognize the importance of parent-child bonding, and do not require the near immediate return to work of the new parent.

- Remote working is the reality of the working world today. Evidence clearly shows that employees working from home are more productive, more loyal, less distracted and less stressed. If you don't see remote working as an advantage in this day and age, you are missing a huge opportunity.

WORKPLACE ENVIRONMENT

- Someone who is not part of an organization's leadership is most certainly not working in a private space. Offering a dedicated place or "quiet room" where employees can have a moment of privacy if they are feeling ill, emotionally overwhelmed, or need to make a personal call can decrease early departures, shorten break times, help de-escalate a situation, and increase an employee's sense of being cared for.

- Social spaces such as lounges, gaming stations, foosball tables, and other sources of entertainment also go a long way to strengthen team cohesion, release stress and offer some activity without leaving the premises. This would be introduced only after all the other substantive changes are made,

- A kitchen (with places to eat together) allows people to bring in healthy and cost-effective meals prepared at home, and encourages positive social connections outside the employee's immediate circle.

FINANCIAL SUPPORT

- Providing a small-loan program with no interest so that employees struggling with cash flow issues can manage from paycheck to paycheck.

- Providing employees with a way of consolidating or restructuring their student loan and other debt. This is huge for employees who are drowning in a sea of debt.

- Bulk or discounted purchasing that offer reduced rates on personal items that are required by employees such as cellphones and childcare, or legal assistance for those that are struggling with legal issues that could ultimately bankrupt them.

HEALTH CARE SUPPORT

- Providing health insurance plans with low or no deductibles so that employees are able to proactively take care of their health, which ultimately benefits the organization.

- During times when an employee is experiencing a health crisis (personally or with an immediate family member), we know that health-related expenses can quickly consume all savings and plunge a person into unmanageable debt. Temporary financial assistance during a health crisis provides instant relief to one area of crushing pressure so that the person can concentrate on dealing with the illness. The payback rate for these loans is almost 100% and the loyalty you foster - priceless.

THE HALLMARK OF A PRE-EMPTIVE STRIKE LEADER

There is nothing revolutionary about these ideas - only that a revolution is required in leadership that recognizes the time is upon us and we must respond to a workforce that is very different from the ones that have come before. True leadership will recognize the sea change and take advantage of the opportunity to transform their organizations in ways that will leave them thriving for decades to come.

The behavior that engenders the emotionally safest workplace for employees is one where the person in charge leads as a steward, rather than as an executive or manager. True leaders operate from a place of understanding human behavior and interpersonal relationships; they foster and facilitate communication and interactions that are open and welcoming. Leaders make decisions that consider the whole, and not just the pieces. Leaders model behavior that communicates to everyone that they are valued. Leaders don't manage people; they motivate them. Leaders take a bottom-up approach instead of top-down. Leaders are not rigid or myopic and do not demand structure and compliance. Leaders take the long view and recognize that to create a culture of emotional safety is to create an organization that has the least risk, liability, cost and distraction.

So, ask yourself the question - what kind of leader are you?

Are you slamming the window of tolerance shut on your employees and driving up your organizational risk to catastrophic levels, or are you throwing open the windows so your employees can breathe and you can experience the delicious smell of success?

LEADING THE TROJAN HORSE TO PASTURE

This book is all about the conditions that exist inside our workplaces that are creating liability, cost, risk and distraction each and every day. As leaders of our organizations, we need to recognize and appreciate the fact that there are loaded Trojan Horses wheeling into our offices every day. We call them employees.

As stated at the outset of this book, employees don't start out as our enemies, they just come equipped with the propensity for it. It's right there, packed into their horses in the form of external stressors, unrealistic expectations, crippling relationships with power, and reactions to triggers at the hands of their stand ins. When we add employer triggers into the mix, our once optimistic and productive employees transform into our greatest nightmares.

We cannot change the Trojan Horse that has wheeled into our workplace; we need our employees. But we can absolutely determine a course of action based on our own organizational behavior that can dramatically reduce the likelihood that we are going to provoke our employees to start unloading their horse shit all over our office.

In this day and age, we cannot afford to be actively creating an army of resentful troops through the mismanagement of our employees. Accusations no longer have to be accurate – only inflammatory. Thanks to the internet and social media, the court of public opinion will have us tried, found guilty, and executed before we wake up.

So, do you want to keep traveling down this road? Our assumption is that if you are reading this book, there must be something going on in your organization that is motivating you to look for answers, and hopefully you've found some here. At a minimum, you should be a lot clearer about the reality of what's going on with your employees and, more importantly, your managers. But what we really hope is that you have found a tool for understanding, analyzing, and totally annihilating the behavioral threats that have infiltrated your organization.

Time to put those horses out to pasture!

PRE-EMPTIVE STRIKE CONSULTING

preemptivestrikeconsulting.com

It only takes one disgruntled employee to topple the empire. Our job is to help ensure you don't end up at the bottom of the pile of rubble.

The authors, Dr. Arlene Battishill and Michael Levitt, can be found at the Los Angeles and Toronto based Pre-Emptive Strike Consulting firm.

Pre-Emptive Strike Consulting (preemptivestrikeconsulting.com) is the only leadership and training firm that deals exclusively with the risk associated with behavioral issues in the workplace.

PESC draws on its founders' decades of experience in leadership positions, human resources, organizational development, behavioral analysis, interaction analysis, and employee stress analysis.

PESC offers several different risk assessment, interpretation, training and consulting programs to organizations of all sizes (preemptivestrikeconsulting.com/services). No matter the business you're in, you've got employees that represent threats to the long-term viability of your organization and if you're not treating those threats seriously and responding with a robust pre-emptive strike plan, you're leaving your organization and yourself in a profoundly compromised position.

The PESC STRAP tool (Sensitivity and Tolerance Risk Assessment Program) referenced in the book can be found at preemptivestrikeconsulting.com/STRAP.

PESC also offers the Pre-Emptive Strike Training Certification for professionals who are seeking to help their own organizations deal with behavioral threats and those who are interested in expanding their own "book of business" or opening up new opportunities for consulting. For more information, go to preemptivestrikeconsulting. com/certification.

CPSIA information can be obtained
at www.ICGtesting.com
Printed in the USA
LVHW081631090119
603300LV00009B/234/P

9 781640 854949